The Adornment of Gods

The Adornment of Gods

Rare Objects from the *Amrapali Jewels Museum*

DEVDUTT PATTANAIK

First published by Westland Books, a division of Nasadiya Technologies Private Limited, in 2022

No. 269/2B, First Floor, 'Irai Arul', Vimalraj Street, Nethaji Nagar, Allappakkam Main Road, Maduravoyal, Chennai 600095

Westland and the Westland logo are the trademarks of Nasadiya Technologies Private Limited, or its affiliates.

Photography by Umesh Gogna
Styling by Prateeksha K. Tholia
Author's photograph by Harpreet Chhachhia.

Devdutt Pattanaik asserts the moral right to be identified as the author of this work.

ISBN: 9789395073363

10 9 8 7 6 5 4 3 2 1

Design by Saurabh Garge
Typesetting by Jojy Philip

Printed at Thomson Press (India) Ltd

Contents

SECTION V: GODS

Foreword

Since the very beginning of Amrapali's journey into the realm of jewellery and jewelled objects, we observed a surfeit of motifs and designs that spoke to us beyond their literal meaning. The trajectory of Indian thought and philosophy that influenced these design details slowly became evident to us as did the narratives planted by people who helped us source these wondrous treasures. In contemporary India, rapid modernisation has meant that the histories and stories of many of these objects are slowly being forgotten. What is fading from public memory is both the use of these objects and awareness about what they depict.

A civilisational strength of the subcontinent has been the continuity of its narrative traditions. Especially our many myths and their depictions across material culture. The gods, goddesses and their stories did not just provide a passive historical narrative but were frequently invoked across an individual's rite of passage. These momentous occasions are thus celebrated using jewellery and sacred objects which conjure divine presence through symbols, sacred forms and, very often, a depiction of the gods. This book is the first to celebrate the intricate relationship between India's mythology and her jewelled arts.

Over the past few years, we have been observing Devdutt Pattanaik's deliberations on the myths and legends of India. His ability to distil their meaning and convey the import of this wealth of intangible heritage in the simplest ways greatly appealed to us. Could he explain the symbolism and lore that are frequently depicted and invoked across hundreds of objects in our collection? This book that you hold in your hands is the fruit of our queries to him. In these pages are answers to things that have perplexed us and meanings we have struggled to understand. And they are all now in a form that allows us to share them with the wider world—an outreach challenge we set ourselves up for when the Amrapali Jewels Museum at Jaipur, Rajasthan, was instituted.

The fifty objects that Devdutt expands on are but a small sample of the holdings at Amrapali Jewels Museum and the founder's family collection. They are, however, representative of our collection at its conceptual widest. From the five elements that have wrought creation, to the subcontinent's myriad gods and goddesses, our plentiful flora and fauna, to objects intrinsic to religious rites and rituals, votive offerings, jewellery and decorative objects, this book covers a vast narrative that no single thread could otherwise hold. While silver is the base material across almost everything you will experience here, gold and other precious materials frequently animate the narrative.

Historically, the consumption of silver and gold across the subcontinent has been termed insatiable over millennia. The constant repurposing of objects and melting them down to their base metal has been a perennial issue across our culture. Consequently, while we might see the evolution of design, shape and forms, we are sadly left with very few objects of the past. The Amrapali Museum's effort has been to safeguard and help preserve this historic legacy wherever possible. No example was considered too small, meagre or unimportant in our collecting mandate if it provided a strong enough connection and helped us understand our past. The collection today offers unique entry points to the vast wealth of creative skills that we have inherited. The range of techniques and traditions, shapes and scales, besides aesthetic choices that transform an object as it moves across time and its realms of use, have guided us in this endeavour to capture our history and culture in the form of objects.

We thank Devdutt for having made this book a reality, and for enabling our collection to be seen in a new light, especially by a younger audience whose reference points might otherwise remain only in the realm of curiosities. We hope that this book arouses an appreciation of our material culture, their many makers across geographies, their uses, layered meanings and, finally, their continued ability to engage with us today.

Rajesh Ajmera and Rajiv Arora

The following abbreviations have been used to specify the dimensions of the objects:

H: Height, W: Width, D: Depth,

Dia: Diameter, uDia: Upper diameter, lDia: Lower diameter

elements

earth

Hindu gods are often placed on thrones, known as asan or pidha. But the throne is not just a place to sit–it represents the earth, one of the primal elements. It also represents the realm of humans: above is the celestial realm of the devas and below the mysterious subterranean realm of the nagas and asuras. If the throne represents the earth, the umbrella above it represents the sky, and the footstool below it represents the nether regions overpowered by the king or deity.

The throne is rectangular or square to indicate domesticated earth, that belongs to humans. It is the kshetra, or space, over which humans have dominion, kshatra. Nature is represented by a circle. This is so even in Chinese mythology. The circle represents the expanse of nature, while the square represents the restraint of culture. Made square, the wild earth is now converted into a piece of human property. Hence the seat of the gods, and kings, is always square.

The four directions are the cardinal directions: north, south, east, west. The corners represent the ordinal directions. Typically, the seating is done in such a way that the throne or the seat always faces the rising sun, the east. The setting sun should fall behind the throne, the west. So the deity feels the first ray of the sun, a symbol of growth. The devotee, facing the deity, is protected from the setting sun, a symbol of decay.

The moment you are facing the east, your left hand is facing the north. Therefore, the north is called Vama. Vama is the left side. This is often reserved for the goddess if the deity is presented as a conjugal pair (maithuna). The south is represented by the right hand, so the right hand is called the southern hand or the Dakshina hand.

This is where Vastu-shastra or Hindu geomancy, that gives meaning to directions, comes to play. Every direction has a deity who enables and empowers the king or deity seated on the throne. The king, or deity, sits facing the east. That's the direction of Indra, the god of rain. His back is kept by Varuna, the god of the sea. On his left side, is Kuber, the god of treasures. On the southern side is the god of death, Yama. So, there is gain on one side and the other side is loss. This is how balance is being maintained. You have the rising sun, the setting sun, the northern treasures of the living and the southern realm of the dead. The king's job is to maintain balance. The square and the throne represent the earth and the balance maintained on earth. Consequently, they represent rajdharma, or governance. The square not only represents human property but also the balance of nature and culture, growth and de-growth and life and death. Using contemporary vocabulary, we can say the throne reminds the king or deity of the balance between cultural needs and nature's limitations, development, and sustainability.

Asan/ Throne
Silver gilded, enamel, pearls, glass beads
19th century, western India
H-185, W-70, D-55 mm

Miniature throne and parasol, silver enamelled in blue, green and brown against a gilded backdrop. Details depict cows, fishes and peacocks on the front with the three remaining sides and the top of the parasol decorated with floral patterns. Flower motifs mark the position on the seat where the deity would be placed when in use. The distinct water ripple pattern on the seven finials and other vegetal design elements indicates a western Indian provenance. Cultures where water was hard to come by often invoked it by visual imagery in arts and crafts. The scale of the object and designs featured indicate its use for a Krishna idol in a devotee's personal shrine.

sky

The moment the earth is represented by a throne, the sky (akash) is represented using the umbrella (chhatri). You find this even in the Sikh gurudvaras where the holy book (Granth Sahib) is placed on a special throne (takhth), fusing the seat the umbrella into one unit. The king is often called the Chhatrapati, the one who sits under the umbrella.

The umbrella is the sky over the king's dominion. So, it is often decorated by the sun, the moon, the stars, the twenty-eight Nakshatras (the lunar asterisms) or the zodiac (the twelve astrological signs). The grahas are the sun and the moon and the five visible planets, i.e. Mercury, Mars, Jupiter, Venus and Saturn, which are the days of the week and, of course, Rahu and Ketu. Rahu is associated with eclipse and Ketu with comets. The stars make up the zodiac rashi or the lunar asterisms, which are the Nakshatras. So, the movement of the stars is placed on the chhatri. The chhatri becomes the symbol of the sky. It also embodies the grace and the protection of the devas, Vedic gods who live in the sky.

In the Vedas, the sky is Dyaus. The earth is Prithvi. The relationship between the sky and the earth is that of the father and the mother, which is a common theme across many mythologies. It is said that the earth and the sky were once together. In the Vedic context, Indra separates the two and brings wind and the clouds between them. This is the atmosphere (antariksha). In the Vedic period, these were the three worlds. In the Vedic period, there is no reference to the underworld or Patala. Patala, as a concept, emerges in the Puranic period. The three Vedic worlds are the earth, the sky and the atmosphere in between.

Portable shrine

Gold, rubies, pearls, rudraksha seeds

18th century, south India

a) H-155, W-133, D-65 mm

b) H-105, W-75, D-10 mm

c) H-36, W-40, D-14 mm

In sharp contrast to Vishnu's aniconic form as a Shalagrama (ammonite) stone, the shrine that houses it is profusely decorated with precious materials. The stone, now removed, would have been placed within the golden receptacle seen on the ruby-encrusted and pearl-festooned plinth. The plinth rests on four legs sculpted to resemble mythic yalis or leogryphs. Just above the Shalagrama box is the serpent Shesha's hoods fanned in protection. The ornamental Prabhavali, indicating the presence of a divine halo is etched in gold repoussé surmounted by a Kirtimukha or glorious face. The cusped arch architrave springs from composite elephant and bird motifs. Detachable pennants called Lanchana and Patake are offerings to the deity, alluding to the devotee's urge to conquer ego by submitting to the god's banner or flag. A parasol topped by a lotus bud and a pearl fringe surmounts the icon. The shrine, part of a devotee's suite, includes a ruby-encrusted gold Vishnu Pada (feet), and a rosary of sixteen rudraksha seeds, encased in gold. The design and style of workmanship indicates a provenance from south India.

wind

When you have the Chhatri or umbrella representing the sky above, and the throne representing the earth below, and the footstool as the subterranean region, between them is the wind. How do you represent the wind, Vayu, or Maruta, the storm, using art? The wind-god or Vayu is sometimes visualised riding a deer, but more likely he is depicted as either a fan or the flag. Hanuman, the son of the wind god, Vayu, is frequently invoked on temple flags. In other instances he is seen on Arjuna's banner and is referred to as Kapi Dhvaja.

Vishnu is identified with the Garuda-dhvaja—the flag with the eagle-like figure carrying the pot of amrit, or nectar of immorality. Vishnu wanted Garuda to be his mount. Garuda said, 'I want to be placed both below you and above you.' So, Vishnu made him both his vahana (mount below him) and his dhvaja (symbol above him).

The most common fans used are the chanwar or the the yak's tail fly-whisk, the morcha, which is made with peacock feathers. The yak's tail fly-whisk is associated with kings and gods, while the peacock feather fan is for the ministers and viziers. In Hindu mythology, Ram is king and so entitled to the chanwar, while Krishna who is not king but part of a confederacy is given a morcha.

The flag, i.e. dhvaja or pataka, could be square-shaped or of a triangular shape (pennant). Often placed atop thrones and temple domes, flags carry distinct symbols. In the case of gods, their vahana, or mount, doubles up as the symbol on their flags. So, Shiva has the bull symbol; Vishnu has the eagle; Brahma has the swan; and Ganesha has the rat. Similarly, dynasties of kings, too, have distinct symbols. For instance, the Suryavamshis, or the solar dynasty of kings to which Ram belongs, have the sun on their pennant while the Chandravamshis, the lunar dynasty to which Krishna belongs, have the moon.

Temple flags
Silver
19th century, western India
H-112, W-51, D-10 mm; H-90, W-60, D-10 mm

Portable shrines were miniature approximations of temples and usually detailed down to their important iconographic elements. These silver flags, shaped in joint pennant form, depict Hanuman and Garuda. The Hanuman flag is an example of pierced silver work whereas the Garuda image has been created by the repoussé and chasing technique. Both flags are attached to longer cylindrical poles that would fit into precise slots on the shrine structure and were possibly a Vaishnava worship object. Both Hanuman, son of the wind god Vayu, and the winged Garuda, Vishnu's mount, are Vaishnava symbols and invoked as flags because of their association with air, one of the Pancha Maha-Bhoota or five great physical elements, the basis of all creation in Hinduism.

water

The sea-god, Varuna, is visualised riding a dolphin; the sky-god, Indra, who brings rain, is visualised riding a white elephant with seven trunks, while the river-goddesses are visualised riding dolphins, turtles and fishes. The river-goddesses hold pots in their hands.

Water can be represented symbolically by using the lotus flower. It can also be represented using the conch shell. The conch shell represents the sea, as we know the conch is a sea creature. But the most important symbol of water is the fish. Fish, conch shell and lotus indicate water out there in nature. Pots also indicate water, but pots are an artificial creation. Only humans create it. Pots indicate proprietorship over water. The ability to carry water and so travel away from a water source for long periods of time. An archaeologist, when he finds a pot shard, knows he has found human civilisation. It indicates the human ability to invent and control nature. Pots indicate the use of human imagination. While all animals go to the water to drink, we have a pot to collect water and carry it with us. So, the pot is considered a symbol of personal property–'It's my water.' Therefore, the pot is worshipped in India as a goddess.

The word for pot is Kumbha. It is also the symbol of the womb. All life comes from the womb. If you look at the uterus, it looks like a pot. So, the pot is closely associated with the goddess, the womb and personal wealth. The earliest known representation of gods in India used pots. The pot would contain water, grain, fruits, vegetables, pulses and cereals. It would be overflowing with leaves, like the mango and the banana leaf. On top of it, you would have a coconut and bananas. These are all fertility symbols. This overflowing pot would be placed on the ground or on a pile of rice, and you would worship it.

Today, people keep asking whether there were temples in ancient days. In ancient days, they didn't have temples. They didn't have gods' images. They would create the god using the pot containing food and water, and worship it with lamps. After the worship, the image would be removed. So, there remained no trace of the deity. This practice continues even today.

If you look at Buddhist, Jain and Hindu motifs, across geographies, and at all the Sanatan symbols, you will find the pot: symbol of food, fertility, abundance, and wealth.

The basic form of this ritual flask is seen worldwide with double volute ends surrounding a central column where the container is filled. The swan neck and beaked spout has a cap attached to the body of the flask by way of multiple chains, securing the piece from loss while adding a touch of whimsy to the object. The silver container is decorated along all its edges with a gilded repoussé vegetal scroll that terminates in designs depicting Gandeberunda (the two-headed bird), emblem of the former Mysore State, and Nandi, Shiva's bull. Note the cap's hinge that ends its curve in two delicate lotus buds. This portable silver vessel was believed to be therapeutic besides keeping water cool and would have been a ceremonial royal commission for a seer.

Ritual flask
Silver, parcel-gilt
19th century, Mysore, south India
H-260, W-240, D-87 mm

fire

Humans are the only living creatures who have domesticated fire. Fire of this earth contained by a lamp (deepa), or the fire-altar (yagna-kunda) and the hearth or the kitchen fire (chulha).

Fire is one of the primal elements, the first deity to be acknowledged by the Vedas, as it connects the earth through the atmosphere to the sky, i.e., the celestial realms. Vedas says that the sun is the fire in the sky, lightning is the fire of the middle world and the fire that we burn is the fire of the earth. The invisible fire under the earth is the volcano. The fire, which is within our body, is our spirit, or soul (the atma).

Fire needs to be understood both literally (element) and metaphorically (soul). The thing about fire is that, unlike the earth, sky, water and wind, it needs fuel. It consumes. However, unlike a plant or an animal it doesn't look for food, which means it doesn't have Jeeva or life. It is a being that is non-living yet living, not seeking food but needing food to stay aflame, a liminal being, connecting the gods to humans.

Animals run from forest fire. Humans controlled it, even generated it, and kept it contained using the torch, the lamp, the fire-altar, the hearth and the kitchen fire. In the Vedic period, the yagna-kunda was used to invoke the gods; it was kept on the northern side. The kitchen fire was used for the house; it was kept on the eastern side. Because ancestors appeared at night, you lit the lamp at dusk. They kept away demons. Demons (rakshasa) and ghosts (preta) could be ancestors (pitr). Ancestors are respected but not welcomed home. Hence, the lamp helped. In old days, it was the torch, but the more civilised societies would use lamps of clay and oil or ghee. Oil was made from plants (coconut, sesame, mustard) and ghee from milk of cows, goats and buffaloes. Kitchen fire used cow-dung cakes. Yagna fire used wood and ghee. Lamps took ghee or plant oils. The more we understand fire as the indicator of human civilisation, the more we understand Vedic civilisation and the Vedic way of thinking.

Oil Lamp
Silver
20th century, north India
H-307, W-270, D-65 mm

This elaborately framed oil lamp with a single wick is frequently seen in iron and other metal forms across several communities in north India. This rare silver example is four-tiered with its back surmounted by flanking peacocks that taper to a hook and help it hang. Each tier ends in a bird head silhouette with bells on their beaks. The cusped arch cut-outs are strung with three dangling leaves and are punctuated by flower heads at regular intervals. A focal point that would emerge when lit would be Ram's head on the lamp's central axis. The base ends with bells that would tinkle when moved with light. This silver lamp, with low relief chasing and engraving, takes on several shapes in the region and possibly harks back to its tribal origin. Indian design often invokes flanking peacock motifs as a decorative device for balance and symmetry.

sun

The sun is a common motif in Hindu art. When paired with the moon, it represents time or eternity. The sun is called Aditya, the son of Aditi, who is one of the many wives of Kashyapa. Kashyapa descends from Brahma, who is the creator of all living organisms of the world. Thus, the sun is seen as an organism, not an object. He sees us just as we see him. In Japanese myths, the sun is female, the goddess Amaterasu, but in Hinduism, Buddhism and Jainism, the sun is male.

The sun is visualised as riding a chariot from east to west every day. This chariot has twelve wheels to represent the twelve zodiacs and seven horses to represent the seven days of the week. The sun's charioteer is the god of dawn, who is of indeterminate gender, sometimes male (Aruna) and sometimes female (Usha). In some stories, the sun god's mother first gave birth to a malformed child, Martanda, which became the dawn and the dusk. Between dawn and dusk is the perfectly formed sun, sometimes visualised as a bird. There are myths where Martanda and Surya were born of eggs, the first of which was broken prematurely by an impatient Aditi, resulting in a malformed and androgynous child, the dawn.

The sun has two wives, Saranya (sunlight) and Chhaaya (shade). Unable to bear the radiance of the sun, Saranya ran away from her husband's house leaving behind her double, the shadow. When Surya realised it, he followed his wife, asked his father-in-law to reduce a portion of his radiance and reconciled with his wife. The sun's father-in-law used the extra portion of the sun's radiance to make weapons for the gods.

Both wives of Surya gave birth to many children. Two such children are Manu, the first living being, and Yama, the first to die. From Manu come all living beings. Yama rules the land of the dead and watches over the dead who await rebirth. The sun is also the father of the Ashwin twins, who ride horses and are linked with the morning and evening star.

Surya goes on many adventures. His greatest enemy is the eclipse known as Rahu. Surya is also Indra's enemy, as Indra is linked to rain and hence to clouds and thunder. When the sun becomes too powerful in summer, we pray for rain. When it gets too rainy and wet, we want the sun to come back. In European traditions, the battle is between summer and winter. In Indian traditions, it is between summer and the rains. Many Indian kings trace their lineage to the sun. These are the Suryavamshi or solar kings, the foremost of whom was Ram.

Temple door
Silver
20th century, Kutch, Gujarat/ Rajasthan
H-1550, W-880, D-100 mm

This is a silver-panelled double door set with eight oval cartouche panels. The uppermost register depicts the sun and the moon gods. These are followed by panels with inscriptions: the left one records the door as being installed in Bhuj, Kutch, during the reign of Maharao Khengarji III (1866–1942), and the right documents that it was donated by Prem Bai and her grandsons, in the memory of Prem Bai's late husband Rattanji, and is dedicated to Lord Krishna in his incarnation as Madan Mohan. The four remaining panels depict floral imagery in the finest tradition of silversmithing in Kutch. The borders of the door depict a hybrid style with local decorative elements merging with European patterns. The presence of a crisp, precise, chased scrolling foliage was a local hallmark and much imitated elsewhere. Two round door handles are suspended from the central bar while the panel at the bottom right has a slot for a key to lock the door. Celebrated for their skill, the region's silversmithing tradition was much patronised both in India and by the British in the 19th and early 20th centuries.

रतनजीनी विधवा
बाई प्रेमबाई ए पोताना
पतिना स्मरणार्थे पर
मात्मा श्री मदनमोहन
जीने रूपानां कमाड श्री
कृष्णार्पण कर्यां छे सं १९
६७ना माघ ॥

॥श्रीमन्महाराजाधिरा
जमिर्जांमहाराओश्री
७खेंगारजीसवाईब·
हादुरजी·सी·आई·ई·
नासमयमांश्रीभुजनग
रनास्थाईमोढ·अडालजा·
मेताजीवण·

moon

When you show the sun and the moon in Hindu art, people know you are talking about time. The Indian calendar uses the radiant sun and the moody moon to mark time. The sun is used to mark the solstices and equinoxes, which indicate festivals linked to the winter and summer harvests. The waxing and the waning of the moon are used to mark the festivals, a model that existed long before the 'week' model was introduced to India by the Greeks. Most festivals are held in the waxing period and very few in the waning period.

Time in Indian mythology is divided into a bright half and a dark half. So, the day has a bright half marked by the sun and a dark half marked by the moon. The month has a bright half and the dark half, as the waxing and the waning moon, respectively. The year has a bright half as the sun moves in the northern direction, Uttarayan, and a dark half as it moves in the southern direction, Dakshinayan. Time is continuously being measured using light, sun and moon.

The moon god is visualised riding a chariot pulled by deer. Deer symbolise the mind, restless and timid, and the moon is also connected with moods and emotions. As the ancients discovered, the moon somehow controls the mind. In fact, lunatic, the English word for an insane or eccentric person, has its etymological root in 'Luna', the Latin word for moon. In Nepali art, the moon sometimes rides a chariot driven by geese, who embody the clouds.

Moon is considered to be a very handsome god. It is said that when gods churned the ocean of milk, male beauty emerged in the form of the moon god. Such was his beauty that Tara, the star goddess, wife of Brihaspati, eloped with him and produced the child Budh (Mercury). Brihaspati cursed the child to be born of uncertain gender. This is why the mercurial Budh is visualised in Indian art sometimes as male and sometimes as female. From Budh are born kings who trace their lineage back to the moon.

There are twenty-seven lunar asterisms in the sky, which the Vedic astronomers identified as Nakshatra. Just as Western astrology divides the sky into twelve compartments, Indian astrologers divided the sky into twenty-seven compartments marked by these Nakshatras. These Nakshatras are the wives of the moon god, but his favourite among them was Rohini. Because the moon god preferred one over the rest, the other wives complained to their father, Daksha, a son of Brahma, who cursed the moon to lose his glow. Hence the moon began to wane, they say. To survive this, Chandra went to Shiva, who placed him on his forehead and so the moon began to wax once again. The waxing and the waning moon represent the tension between Daksha and Shiva, the rivalry between the Vedic and the Tantric traditions, respectively, besides marking time, kingship and moods.

Kappu/ Half-moon pendant
Silver
19th century, Malabar, Kerala
H-44, W-113, D-13 mm

Popular in Calicut, on the Malabar coast, this half-moon silver amulet pendant depicts distinct patterns in curvilinear lines along multiple registers ending with a rounded scroll incorporating fine filigree and granulation techniques. The top shows a cluster of loops (twenty-eight in number) that would enable a metal chain or cord to pass through.

While sometimes worn on the neck, they were mostly attached to waist belts for everyday use and adorned frequently by Kathakali performers. The pattern invokes a design aesthetic with links to Southeast Asia, a region with which the Malabar coast has had long and historic trade relations.

Life

plants

Plants are a very sacred motif. They represent the abundance of nature. They also serve as metaphors for metaphysical ideas. Some plants are more sacred than others. Vishnu is linked to the tulsi plant, Shiva to the bilva plant, Krishna to the kadamba, the Goddess to neem and tamarind, and Ganesha to sugarcane. The gods are also associated with orchards and woods. Shiva, for example, is linked to the deodar forest.

The mango, apart from making the otherwise awful summer delightful, is also considered a very sacred plant. The form of the mango fruit lends to the paisley shape. If you look at it carefully, it appears like a footprint of Lakshmi, the goddess of wealth and fortune. She is celebrated in Hinduism, Jainism and also in Buddhism. Therefore, the aam chhap or the mango motif is very popular.

Flowers are important because they are associated with love and desire. They bloom. They contain nectar and fragrance to attract birds, bees and butterflies, which enables the plants to get pollinated. Flowers are a sexual symbol, and Hinduism acknowledges it very openly. The lotus which blooms in sunlight, is a metaphor for love, arousal and desire for a beloved; here, the sun is the beloved. Similarly, the moon is the beloved for the lotus flowers that bloom at night.

When you show a flower, it represents desire. When you show a leaf or a fruit, it represents food. Flowers and fruits are kept next to each other. Flowers mean that desire has been aroused and you are welcoming the beloved. Fruits represent the fulfilment of the desire. Among the metaphors used in Indian poetry are the beej (seed) and the phal (fruit). The seed of desire manifests as a fruit. Divinity is also associated with these metaphors.

Vishnu, the one who engages with the world, is associated with flowers, fruits and leaves. Around Vishnu's neck, you will find the Vanamali, a garland, with dew-drenched, forest flowers, leaves from the tulsi and the lotus. Meanwhile, Shiva, the mendicant, the austere one, is always associated with the seed, the potential.

Seeds, leaves, flowers and fruits represent two ends of a spectrum. This is how plants are used in motifs to explain concepts. When you see a plant in an artwork, it is not just decorative, it is an idea. The seed represents potential. The leaves represent the yearning for the sun, the food. The flower represents desire. The fruit represents the fulfilment of the desire. This is what separates the organic from the inorganic.

Pichkari/ Water pump
Silver gilded
19th century, western India
H-248, W-102, D-42 mm

This traditional water pump in silver is elegantly decorated across two parts, the tubular front and receding piston. Formal vegetal patterns in the repoussé and chasing techniques are visible on the external tube with both ends tipped in stylised domed caps with pineapple design. The tip of the pump is shaped like an open lotus with tiny perforations to disperse water with the base ending in the rounded grip of the moving piston. Two additional finger grips around the central panel end in mythical maḳara heads regarded as water guardians in sacred rivers. Water gave life to nature and hence the depiction of vegetal motifs on this water pump. Miniature water pumps were popular accoutrements in shrines to depict nativity scenes from Krishna's childhood at Vrindavan. They were used symbolically by priests and devotees to celebrate Holi with Krishna's idol.

fish

Fish is a common motif in Indian art. Found in Jain, Buddhist and Hindu traditions, it is a symbol of auspiciousness. A pair of fish is considered to be a symbol of fertility, of life, of energy. It is associated with movement. A bowl containing two fish was part of many traditions, such as wedding ceremonies. A rich household was one which had a household pond, full of fish to feed the family. So, the fish was always seen as a sign of plenty and positive energy.

A fish also symbolises a fundamental Sanatan (or eternal) concept known as Matsyanyaya, which literally means fish justice. What it relates to, in English, is the law of the jungle, where the strong feed on the weak. That is the nature of the jungle and we don't consider it immoral. Similarly, the big fish eat the small fish, and it is not a crime. But, in human society, where the strong exploit the weak, it is considered to be immoral. So, Matsyanyaya is normal and allowed in the jungle, but not in society. Matsyanyaya in society is Adharma. In a civilised society, the strong take care of the weak. Therefore, matsya, or the fish motif, is a recurring theme in Hindu mythology.

In Brahmana literature, the small fish comes to Manu, the founder of humanity, or the first human, and says, 'Save me from the big fish.' This story is the indicator of the birth of civilisation, for Manu takes the small fish and shelters it in a pot. The human being uses his capability to protect the weak, represented by the small fish, from the big fish, which represents the powerful and the privileged. Human civilisation is thus born.

In the Vishnu Purana, the fish is seen as an avatar of Vishnu, who is teaching Manu the laws of dharma. Later, we are told that there is a great flood, and Manu is saved by a big fish. The fish that he had rescued when it was small and helpless had now become a big fish. The fish rescued Manu when he, in turn, was helpless. Thus, reciprocity is seen. The strong protects the weak. And when the circle of life takes a turn, the weak become strong, the strong become weak, and the courtesy is reciprocated. This is the origin of the concept of dharma, where the fish plays a very important role.

Fish is also associated with desire and sexuality. There are many stories in

Hindu mythology where, when the stomach of the fish is cut open, people find celestial babies inside. There is a story of how Krishna's son, Pradyumna, is kidnapped by a demon called Shambara. He throws the baby into the sea. A fish eats the baby and when a fisherman cuts open the fish, the baby is miraculously still alive. This is how Pradyumna is rescued.

A similar story is told in the Mahabharata. Fishermen cut open a fish to find within it a boy and a girl—Satyavati and her brother. Satyavati is raised by the fisherfolk and becomes the matriarch of the Pandavas and the Kauravas. So, fish is again associated with babies and with fertility.

Many heroes, in Ramayana and Mahabharata, are famous for their marksmanship. They can easily shoot the eye of a fish with an arrow. Here again, a fish becomes a symbol of a target. A lot of attention is paid to the eye of the fish because a fish doesn't blink; it sees all the time. That is another reason why the fish is considered auspicious—not only because it moves but also because its eye is unblinking.

Incense holder
Gold, red-coloured glass
19th century, Odisha
H-113, W-26, D-17 mm

This articulated fish with red-coloured glass eyes and external fins is made of delicately engraved gold rings and is fastened in sections, which helps the object move from side to side. Variously used across the Indian subcontinent for perfume and for kohl (eye make-up), the hinged head opens to reveal an inner compartment which, in turn, is topped by a tiny screw cap. Minute details like the use of twisted gold wire to depict barbels would have delighted its user who would be privy to such minutiae. The fish motif was invoked in design to symbolise abundance and plentifulness, bringing prosperity to communities and, as a mark of independence, of being beyond anyone's control.

tiger

The tiger is native to India. It was especially popular in 18th-century Mysore because of Tipu Sultan who was considered the Tiger of Mysore. Images of the tiger are found in Harappan seals, where we see either a goddess or a hero fighting tigers. This is very much like it was in Mesopotamia, where you had Gilgamesh fighting lions. There are also Harappan seals where a woman is half-tiger like a sphinx. We don't know what they mean.

Among the popular legends in South India is one of King Rajashekhara of Pandalam and his wife. Since they were childless, the gods gave the king a strong and wise boy to raise as his son. It so happened that the moment this boy came to the king's house, the queen became pregnant. The queen resented this adopted son and wanted her biological son to become the king when the time came. So, she hatched a plot.

The queen pretended to be ill and asked her foster son to fetch her the milk of a tigress that would cure her. She hoped that the tigress would kill the boy. However, the boy returned with a herd of tigresses to milk for the queen. That's how he established his divinity. On realising that the queen wanted her biological son to be the king, he renounced the kingdom. He climbed the mountain and became a hermit lord called Ayyappa. Also known as Manikantha, he is pictured riding a tiger. Ayyappa defeated many demons, including the buffalo demon Mahishi.

So, the tiger at one level is the symbol of strength, power and stealth. There are many gods, especially in Goa, Maharashtra and Karnataka, known as Vagoba or Vagya. These are local village gods who have to be appeased so that the tiger does not attack the village.

The goddess is seen riding a tiger. She is called Sherawali or the one who rides the tiger. Tigers are associated with the goddess because cats are generally associated with the goddess. Cats usually take meticulous care of their young. Thus, the goddess is always associated with cats, tigers and lions.

Ornamental tiger
Silver, parcel-gilt
19th century, south India
H-73, W-54, D-19 mm

The large-scale use of silver and other precious materials to create decorative objects as souvenirs seem to have emerged in 19th-century India. This solid cast silver tiger's stance with its head turned back and tongue protruding is meant to give a sense of its potential. Manufactured from a mould and hand-finished by adding detail, the tiger's vertical disruptive colouration stripes are gilded in gold and spread over the body and head. Tiger designs gained popularity after the death of Tipu Sultan (1751–1799) who was known as the Tiger of Mysore. Among the many theories about why he was called so, is one that links it to his famed collection of tiger-patterned objects and accessories.

lion

The lion and the tiger are the two cats of India. The lion no longer exists in India, except in Gir forest in Gujarat; it has otherwise become extinct in the wild. The Gir lions are smaller than African lions, which are gigantic. Whether lions ever existed in India has been a subject of debate. Was the Asiatic lion a real local indigenous species? Or was it imported from the northwest part of India for the sport of kings? This is a controversy for scientists to resolve.

What we do know is that the lion was the symbol of kingship in ancient Egypt and Persia. This idea spread around the world, even to countries where there were no lions. For example, Sri Lanka never had lions, but it has an ethnic community known as the Sinhalese, or the lion people. Similarly, Singapore, which never had lions, is called the City of the Lions. China, too, never had lions, but Forbidden City located in Beijing incorporates the lion motif in its architectural design.

The concept of lion as a symbol of kingship travelled to India, too. We know that the Ashokan Empire was impressed by the Persian Empire. If you see the Ashokan emblem, it has a lion, a horse, a bull and an elephant. The tiger, which is a local animal, is not present. This shows a hierarchy in animals, with kings preferring the lion over the tiger. The local communities in Tamil Nadu, Karnataka, Maharashtra and Goa worship the tiger, the waghya or the puli as it is called in south India.

As far as the goddess is concerned, she is associated with all cats: tigers and lions. Durga is depicted riding into battle on a lion. The earliest known visual representation found in India of the warrior goddess riding a lion dates back to the Kushan period. It likely has linkages to the Mesopotamian or Iranian goddess called Nanna. Associated with both war and love, Nanna rode a lion. She was related to goddesses like Ishtar. While this idea of import is not accepted by all scholars, it is quite plausible that the motif amalgamated with local goddesses who rode tigers and thus became very popular across cultures.

The lion then becomes a symbol of virility and royalty. There are many images of the lion, sitting atop an elephant, in temple art. Lions are also important because we have Vishnu taking the form of a man-lion, a mixture of a man and a lion, in his Narasimha avatar. He does so to kill a demon who could not be killed by either an animal or a human. God was forced to take the form of a monster, or a hybrid beast, neither animal nor human, but a bit of both. He is then able to kill the demon, Hiryanakashipu.

Whenever we see the lion motif, it represents protection. It is associated with the goddess Durga. It is associated with loyalty, royalty and Vishnu's Narasimha avatar. This form of Vishnu was much worshipped in Andhra Pradesh, Karnataka and Odissa. It was associated with kings and kingly power. It then spread to Sri Lanka and Southeast Asia.

Processional sceptre
Silver, parcel-gilt, glass
19th century, western India
H-745, W-268, D-103 mm

This exceptional gilded silver sculpted sceptre is topped by an amber-eyed lion with bared teeth, protruding tongue and defined whiskers. The head crowned by a gilded mane with short curls descends into a coiled vegetal scroll that tapers to a spherical end, punctuated by stylised acanthus foliage bands that hide its joints. Created using multiple processes, the fine detailing exemplifies prevalent skills of repoussé, hammering and silver chasing across western India. Processions in princely India often included sceptres tipped by symbolic and powerful animals, like the lion and elephant, and were part of royal regalia. Known as Lawajama in the north and Biruthus in southern India, the sceptre would also have been used for religious processions.

naga

In Hindu mythology, serpents play a very important role. We are not talking about any serpent. We are talking about Naga, the hooded serpent, well-known as the cobra. The hooded serpent is a symbol of auspiciousness, fertility, mystical power, occult power and magical things. It is a striking contrast against the way the serpent is seen in Abrahamic traditions, where it is a symbol of the devil, a symbol of temptation. A creature that God punishes by making it crawl on its stomach all its life. In Judaism, Christianity and Islam, the serpent is evil. But in Hinduism, it is the symbol of fertility, a symbol of magic.

The serpent lives under the earth. It was believed that the holes it makes reach Patala, the land beneath our feet, and that it had knowledge of how crops germinate and of all the gems of the world. Hence, ancient Indians worshipped serpents as a source of all jewels and fertility. Even today, in the southern parts of India, there are ceremonies known as Nagamandala. Serpent art is drawn on the floor and people invoke the spirit of serpent—serpent gods and goddesses.

Serpents were believed to have shape-shifting abilities. They could turn into humans or become animals. They would live in water. They were associated with abundance and eroticism. There are many stories to that effect. The land of the serpents, under the earth, is called Bhogavati. Its palace is full of jewels. The serpents are believed to have a mani or a jewel embedded in their forehead. This jewel can bring fortune into our lives and cure diseases. Therefore, serpents are invoked for curing ailments as well as to gain beauty and immortality.

The enemy of the serpents is the garuda, or the eagle. There are many images where the two are shown in conflict. Legend has it that serpents were once banned from a kingdom and as soon as they were exiled, there fell a drought. In other words, where there is no snake, there is no rain. So, to bring rain back, the serpents were asked to return. This is why in Buddhism, Jainism and Hinduism, the holy men are shown seated on the coils of a serpent and sheltered by its hood. The image of Buddha when he attains Nirvana and that of Parshunath in Jainism are both with them seated under the hood of a serpent.

Similar stories are found in folklore. There will be a story of an ordinary man sleeping on the ground, and a snake coming and sheltering him from the harsh rays of the sun. That is how the man is identified as a Rajput, the future king. A story goes that when Shankaracharya was travelling across India, he saw a snake. The naga was sheltering a pregnant frog. On that spot, Shankaracharya built a 'math' known as Sringeri math. Snakes are supposed to eat frogs and rats. If they protect them, that place must be auspicious. It is the reversal of the law of the jungle, when the predator protects the prey rather than eating it.

There are various tales about nagas who become humans. In the Ramayana, we have Sulochana, the queen of the nagas, who marries Ravan's son, Meghanada. There are stories of nagas coming to the support of Ram. They enable him to uphold the bridge which is built across to Lanka. In the Mahabharata, Arjun marries the naga princess Ulupi, and they have a son called Iravan.

Nagas are associated with Krishna, too. Krishna defeats the naga Kalia, who has been arrogant and whose venom is destroying the river Yamuna. Kalia's wives, the Nagapatnis, beg Krishna to forgive their husband. We have stories where Vishnu himself lies on the coils of a serpent known as Ananta Shesha or Adishesha. This serpent represents time. Serpent is associated with Shiva, too. Around Shiva's neck sits a cobra. It is called Karkotaka. Another serpent associated with Shiva is Patanjali. This serpent overhears Shiva and thus comes up with the idea of treaties known as Yogasutra, which contains the secrets of Yoga, for humanity. So, you have, with snakes, many worlds emerging: the world of the occult, mysticism, bhakti, devotion and the world of dharma. This makes snakes an integral part of Hindu art.

Pendant
Silver, parcel-gilt
19th century, western India
H-70, W-50, D-12 mm

This austere tribal pendant used as an amulet comes from the culturally rich triangular belt that is spread over Rajasthan, Madhya Pradesh and Gujarat. Using an amulet that invoked a snake was to potentially save the wearer from snake bites. The use of gold to depict the coiled serpent is an unexpected luxury. The pendant was created with fine granulation, soldering, hammering and die-stamping the design on a small silver plate. Traces of resin that has long worn out point to its being cherished by the owner. The tradition of using similar pendants as a protective antidote goes back several millennia and is still in vogue.

birds

One of the key themes of Hindu mythology is antagonism between the predator and the prey. Birds and serpents are always shown as antagonists; the bird fighting with the serpent. They both descend from goddesses and they both have Kashyapa as their father. Kashyapa has two wives, Vinata and Kadru. Vinata is the mother of birds and Kadru is the mother of serpents. There are many stories of why birds and serpents fight with each other. Sometimes, the fight is justified; sometimes, it is not. It really goes to explain the conflict in nature. Humans, however, overcome conflict by collaboration.

In art, when you see a bird, you remember that birds represent the forces in the sky. We always talk of three worlds: the world below the earth, the world on earth and the one above the earth. Humans are located on earth, birds are located in the sky and serpents are located under the earth. Conflict occurs between serpents and birds. Humans stand in the middle of it.
The birds seen in motifs are peacocks, parrots, swans, kites and vultures. The peacock is associated with the warlord Kartikeya. It is a symbol of beauty. It is also associated with Krishna and Shiva. It is the alpha male, surrounded by peahens. So, it becomes symbolic of Krishna and the Maharasa, the gopikas who surround him. It is also symbolic of Shiva who is surrounded by the yoginis.

The parrot is associated with love and desire, with Kamadeva and with Krishna. It is also associated with Suka Muni. Suka Muni is the son of Vyas, the sage who organised all the scriptures, the Vedas. Vyas also composed the Mahabharata, which Suka Muni transmits. This is significant because a parrot is known to memorise and say things without editing it. Therefore, Suka Muni, the compiler, is the one who parrots wisdom. He transmits it, without adding or subtracting from it, to the next generation.

The swan, or hansa, is a sacred spiritual symbol associated with atma, the soul. The idea of detachment is associated with the swan because even as the swan lives in water, the water does not cling to its feathers. Hansa is associated with the goddess of knowledge, Saraswati, and with Brahma, the creator. Paramhansa is a title given to sages who are jeevamukti. They live in society but are detached from it; they engage with society but do not seek to control it. In ancient times, the swan was also a symbol of love, like the parrot. It transmitted lovers' messages to each other. Nala and Damayanti communicate to each other via the swan. The swan, therefore, at one time, was a romantic image. Over time, though, it has become linked to spirituality, with romance being restricted to the parrot. In many art forms, Krishna goes to war on Garuda, an eagle, but Garuda is depicted as the green-coloured parrot.

One of the earliest Buddhist images of a goddess, from the 7th century, is found in Ellora Caves. In Buddhist art, the peacock is also associated with the goddess Tara and the goddess of learning, Mayamayuri. This is why, even today, the Hindu version of Tara, that is Saraswati, is associated with the peacock.

Saraswati is also associated with the swan, goose and the heron. The goose is said to have miraculous powers. It can separate milk from water, indicating the ability to distinguish and separate knowledge from falsehood. The heron is a symbol of concentration. This is how birds play a very important role in the art motifs in the collection.

Pendant
Silver, parcel-gilt
19th century, Himachal Pradesh
H-158, W-123, D-8 mm

Not visible at first glance is the presence of two paired peacocks that face off on the surface of this pendant. While the golden birds catch our eye, the skilled artisan adds another pair in silver surrounded by carved fretwork composed of details from the bird's anatomy along with minute traces of red enamel for colour. The top of the pendant has five decorated loops that allow for a metal chain or cord to pass through it. At the bottom are nine kinetic trefoil leaf clusters. While details have been sparingly chiselled, soldered and die-stamped onto the piece, the austere design is an exemplar of unknown but virtuoso craftsmanship.

garuda

Garuda is the mighty eagle; some say the kite. He flies from earth, through the sky, to the heavens. In the Vedas, it was known as Suparna, the golden bird or the bird with golden wings, which would travel across the sky and bring Soma from the moon to the earth. Over time, Soma came to be associated with amruta or the nectar of immortality, that belonged to the gods. Only Garuda could travel from earth to Indraloka and fetch amruta from the gods back to earth. In the Puranas, we are told that Garuda not only brought amruta from the land of the gods but also liberated his mother, who was enslaved by the Nagas. The Nagas wanted the nectar of immortality and Garuda was forced to steal it. He, however, managed to return the nectar back to the devas as soon as his mother was set free, before the Nagas had a sip of the potion.

'Why did you not take a sip of nectar yourself?' Indra's younger brother, Vishnu, asked Garuda, who had stolen the nectar from the heavens. To which Garuda replied, 'Because it is not mine to take.' For this response, he was chosen to be the vahana, or mount, of Vishnu. Therefore, in every Vishnu temple across India, we will find images of Garuda, right in front of him. He is often shown as a man, with wings and a beak, holding serpents in his claws. Some believe it to be the image of the rising sun that destroys the serpent of the night, because serpents are associated with the night. So, it is an allegory for a solar myth.

Garuda is known to live in Vaikuntha. They say that when Vishnu is sleeping, it is Pralaya, and that he sleeps on a serpent. But when he wakes up, he leaps on Garuda and goes around the world, solving problems. One of the biggest problems that Vishnu solved was saving the king of elephants, Gajendra, from being drowned by a serpent or a crocodile, depending on which version you read. We are told that the king of elephants was enjoying himself in a lotus pond, when a serpent or a crocodile catches hold of his foot and tries to drag him under water. Gajendra is helpless. No one comes to his rescue, until he calls out to Vishnu, who comes, riding Garuda, to save him.

This motif of Gajendra moksha, or Vishnu riding Garuda and saving Gajendra who is his devotee, is an important one in Hindu art. Thus, Garuda is associated with moksha, or salvation. The entrapment of Gajendra is a metaphor for our entrapment in the material world. How our senses and desires ensnare us in the material world. How, through prayer to Garuda, we can break these bonds. These bonds are like the serpent bond or Nagapasha. They bind us to the earth. We pray to Garuda to break these bonds and help us rise up to Vaikuntha.

In art, Garuda is often visualised as a parrot, especially when Vishnu takes the form of Krishna. Krishna is the only form of Vishnu associated with Garuda. According to a legend from Andhra Pradesh, Narakasura had imprisoned many kings and gods. So, Krishna, accompanied by his wife Satyabhama, rides Garuda to defeat him. In the great battle between the two, Narakasura throws a weapon that, instead of Krishna, strikes Satyabhama. Enraged, she picks up Krishna's mace, Kaumodaki, and throws it at Narakasura. This is how Narakasura, who cannot be defeated by any man, is defeated by a woman. Another story is of Krishna going to war against Banasura, and here, too, he is said to be riding Garuda. In Southeast Asia, a popular motif is of Vishnu riding Garuda, with the latter holding the Nagas in his talons.

Garuda
Silver
19th century, Karnataka, south India
H-132, W-70, D-68 mm

This anthropomorphic miniature Garuda figure is an important element of Vaishnava worship traditions. By the 19th century, an image of the winged god Garuda bent on one knee with hands folded in prayer was perhaps his most famous depiction. This piece created in the lost wax process shows Vishnu's vahan (mount) placed on a rounded pedestal surrounded by a carved Indic leaf pattern over a tiered rectangular plinth. The detailing extends to the rear of the figure with delicate designs delineated and etched over his protruding feet and spread wings. The knob finial of the Garuda was attached to a holy container (samputa), a plate-like vessel where ritual offerings were placed.

hanuman

One of the most popular motifs in Indian art is of Hanuman, the monkey god. He is mightier than all beings put together. Hanuman appears in the epic Ramayana, as an assistant to Ram. Ram is a young prince, exiled to live in the forest for fourteen years. His wife, Sita, accompanies him. The rakshasa king, Ravan, abducts Sita. While Ram is looking for his wife, he encounters Hanuman. Hanuman appears as a peculiar being. He is a 'vanara'. Vanara means a monkey, but it also means a forest dweller. Some people believe that the term 'vanara' is a metaphor for tribal beings. However, this does not matter. In mythology, fantasy, metaphors and allegories blur with each other to communicate a meaning.

Ram, who has no army, raises an army of monkeys with the help of Hanuman. Hanuman not only helps Ram find where Sita is but also helps build a bridge across the sea, so that Ram can attack the city of Lanka and defeat Ravan to liberate Sita. Ram rides into battle on the shoulders of Hanuman. When Ram returns to Ayodhya, after the fourteen-year exile, the vanara who accompanies him is Hanuman. So, Hanuman is the assistant of Ram. He who enables things to happen.

In Vaishnava traditions, while Vishnu is the supreme god, the one who carries out his work is Garuda. When Vishnu takes the form of Ram, his work is done by Hanuman. In many ways, Hanuman and Garuda mirror each other. There are many Vaishnava artworks that show Hanuman and Garuda next to each other. Both represent bhakti, that is, devotion. They represent karma, as they do all the deeds that are supposed to be done on behalf of the gods. So, in a way, one can say that they are secretaries or enablers or viceroys of god.

Most importantly, Hanuman is associated with knowledge and wisdom. He is a poet and a writer. He is a great communicator. He speaks Sanskrit. He is fluent in many languages. He composes songs dedicated to Ram. Hanuman is known as a scribe, who writes the name 'Ram' on stones. He is also a great problem-solver. He solves problems for Ram, and he solves problems for Ram's devotees.

Not only does Hanuman have an intellectual side but he also has an emotional and physical side. He is the great devotee. He is visualised as this gigantic monkey, with mighty arms and limbs. His tail is prehensile; he can catch demons with it. He can crush demons with his feet. He can build a bridge across the sea. He can fly across the ocean, carrying a mountain in his hand. Sometimes, he is shown with one head, sometimes, with five heads and sometimes, with ten heads. He is often shown facing the southern

direction because south is the direction of death. Therefore, he is preventing death from invading civilisation and culture.

So, Hanuman is, in a way, an amulet of good luck, power, strength and protection. Therefore, he is a part of many talismans. He is also shown holding a banner in his hand, which is Ram's flag. He is the embodiment of power but not just brute power. It is power linked with devotion and wisdom.

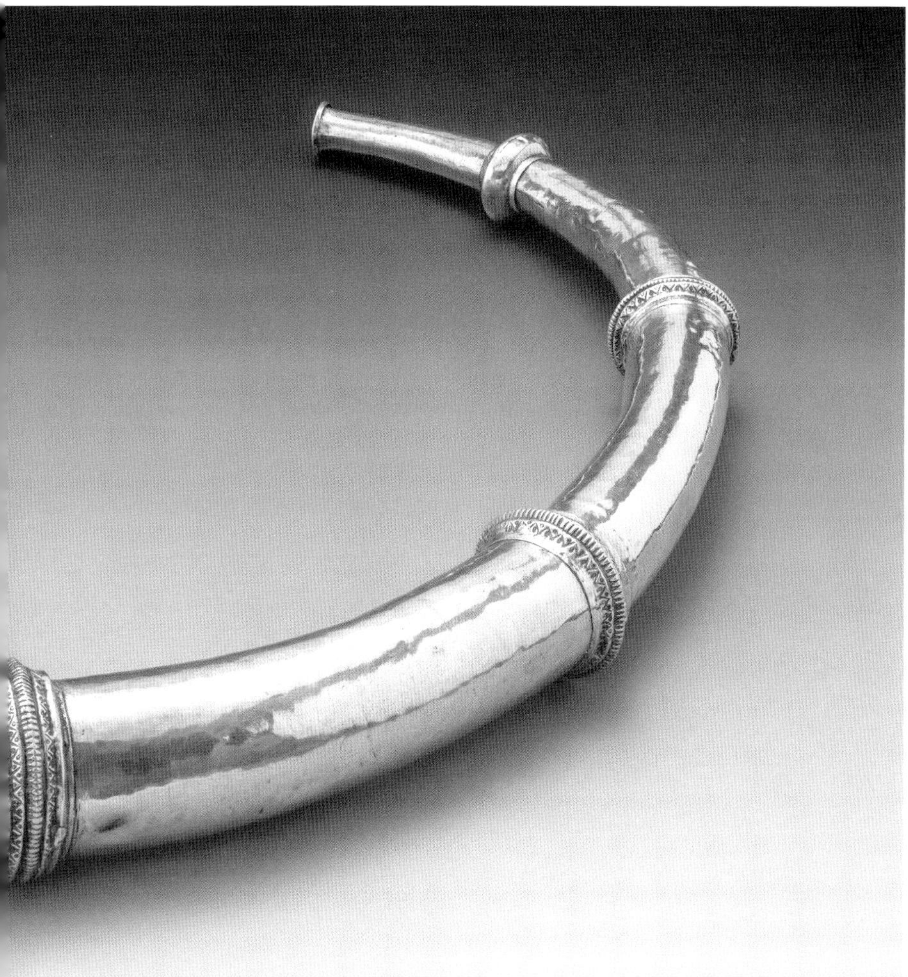

Narsinga trumpet
Silver
19th century, Himachal Pradesh, north India
H-400, W-120, D-32 mm

The popular Narsinga, a C-shaped wind instrument, is seen at religious ceremonies in Himachal Pradesh and Nepal. It is made of two curved tubes that fit into one another forming a crescent. This largely plain silver trumpet that is part of the collection has designs etched around the mouth of its wider end. A detailed inscription just below the mouth is accompanied by a small silver plaque soldered on, which depicts Hanuman retrieving Sanjeevani herbs from the mountains, a popular visual depiction from the Ramayana. Hanuman, the son of the wind god, was often invoked when depicting wind, and the artisan's knowledge of myths and legends frequently added unique flourishes to an otherwise quotidian object.

elephant

In ancient and medieval times, India would export elephants and import horses from other parts of the world. Horses have always been a foreign animal in India. The kings of north-west India controlled the horse trade and were known as Ashwapati. The kings of eastern India had access to elephants and were called Gajapati. Even today, the king of Puri, in eastern India, is called Gajapati.

In the Ramayana and the Mahabharata, you have the kings of Madra, Kaikeya and Gandhara. These regions represent modern Pakistan and Afghanistan, whose kings were called Ashwapati. So, you have these two kinds of worlds that existed. They played a very important role in economics as well as politics.

The elephant became a very sacred animal in India. The prevalence of elephants in the eastern part of India enabled the kings to control the land there. This made them very powerful. In fact, in the Mauryan times, only kings were allowed to own elephants.

Even the Mughal rulers were very careful about who could own elephants. Elephant keepers and elephant stables were marks of royalty. If a king wanted to destroy someone, he would gift them an elephant. Because the upkeep of the elephant cost a lot of money and could drive one to poverty. Even when an elephant died, getting rid of its dead body would cost a lot of money.

The elephant, therefore, became a symbol of power and nobility. This also happened because the elephant is associated with Lakshmi, the goddess of fortune.

Not surprisingly, Indra, the king of heaven, rode an elephant, Airavat. It was a special elephant: it had seven trunks and six pairs of tusks. Indra himself is very interesting. The Vedic Indra is Indo-Aryan. He rides a chariot pulled by horses and there is no reference to elephants. However, the Puranic Indra is associated with elephants.

The first Indian elephant-riding motif comes from Buddhist art. Both the elephant and the horse also find a place in Jain traditions, where the tirthankar Ajitnath is symbolised by an elephant and tirthankar Sambhavnath is associated with the horse.

The elephant is a symbol of power. Rain clouds are equated with the elephant. It is said that the rumbling rain clouds represent the movement of an elephant herd. Literature, thus, has lots of elephant metaphors.

When an elephant is sexually aroused, it is called madhgaja. It becomes the symbol of erotic power. When one becomes a fanatic or a fan and cannot think clearly, it is said that one behaves like a sexually aroused elephant. The word, madira, for alcohol, comes from the word madh or musth. Musth is a secretion from the temporal ducts of an elephant, and it is said to make the elephant aggressive and dangerous. The elephant, therefore, is a symbol of wealth, power, sexual arousal and royalty.

Ornamental object
Silver, parcel-gilt
19th century, western India
H-120, W-86, D-45 mm

In this cast silver ceremonial elephant, caparisoned by a traditional howdah, the animal's body is chiselled to depict its natural striations while elaborate details by repoussé are chased on its trappings—the cloth, the mahout and the large howdah. The details depicted are meant to convey an animal in motion: floral vases on an upturned tusk show the animal's trained status and its ability to stay in equilibrium, while the two tinkling bells indicate the sound the animal would have created while moving. The souvenir market for objects portraying an exotic India was very popular and a vast number of decorative objects were created for this trade in several regional styles and techniques.

bull

The moment you talk of Hinduism, you talk of the cow and the bull. The cows were used for milk and for dung. Cow dung was used as fuel. Milk was used as food. The bull was castrated to become an ox, which would then be used to pull carts and ploughs. If you castrated the bull, it could not reproduce. The virile, uncastrated bull was considered very valuable and sacred. It was a wild creature, kept aside from the tribe. It was used to impregnate the cow, so that she could give milk.

The bull, therefore, was an important motif. Harappan seals have images of the bull and of bull fighting. Moreover, bulls, or Rishbha, are sacred in both Hinduism and Jainism. In Jainism, the bull as Rishabhnath symbolises the earliest sage, Tirthankara Rishabha. In Hinduism, the animal is associated with Shiva and represents the autonomy and the ferociousnes of the wild, untamed god. The bull is always found in front of Shiva temples.

Since the bull is considered sacred in both Hinduism and Jainism, one finds a lot of bull motifs in the iconography in India. The bull is also the symbol of dharma. They say that dharma establishes civilisation—that which differentiates us from animals. The bull's four legs are considered to be the four pillars of dharma. It is said that as time passes, the bull of dharma loses its legs, one by one. So, in the earliest age, it stands on four legs; in the next, it has three; then two and finally, one, before it is swept away by pralaya, the waters of doom. Then, another world regenerates itself as a new bull.

The Zebu bull, which has a large hump, is associated with the Harappan times. It is a native bull of India. It was not brought by the Aryans. The bull was obviously an important animal. We have images of bulls and people jumping over them in Harappa. The practice of Jallikattu in Tamil Nadu today can perhaps be traced to the Harappan civilisation. So, the veneration of cows and bulls is not restricted just to the Aryans but was part of the Harappan civilisation as well. These are the two major tributaries of Hindu thought.

Nandi case
Silver
19th century, Deccan Plateau
H-420, W-480, D-200 mm

Stone figures of Nandi in Shaivite temples face the Shivalinga or idol of Shiva, usually the principal deity in Shaivite shrines. Often, covers for the stone statue were gifted as votive offerings by devotees and displayed on days when special rituals or celebrations were conducted. The two halves of this silver cover are an exact fit to a yet unidentified stone Nandi. The bull's horns, hump and feet are stylised approximations to contain the original stone figure beneath the case. Sparse trapping details are delicately etched onto the surface of this case while a cowherd or Gana is depicted at front holding onto the bull's neck. The Maharashtra–Karnataka border frequently saw the application of sheet silver covers for Shivalingams, folk deities and Nandi.

COW

The cow is one of the most sacred motifs in Hinduism and Jainism. The cow was something that all sages sought. In ancient India, a cow was considered essential for survival. The cow's milk was food and cow dung was used to make fuel for homes. Thus, if a man had a cow, he was self-sufficient. The cow-print (go-pada) was a symbol of arriving auspiciousness and of abundance.

A cow gives you milk all her life. The right thing to do when a cow became old was to not slaughter her. While eating bulls was part of ancient diets, this was later frowned upon and became part of the beef taboo that Hinduism is associated with today.

The cow is always associated with the calf to remind us it is a milk-giving cow. Images of cows are meant to evoke a maternal feeling in the viewer (vatsalyaras). Even the gods had a milk-giving cow called Kamadhenu. Her calf was called Nandini.

You will always find stories where sages would ask kings to give them cows. Over time, it became a metaphor for livelihood and for the earth. The earth is called cow: you take care of the earth, you plough it and you put seeds in it. It will give you crops. You can milk the earth by harvesting it.

The gods have it, the sages have it, the kings have it. The kings are supposed to be the protectors of the cow. As mentioned earlier, there would also be a metaphorical symbolism to this. The king being the guardian of livelihood of the earth was expected to give cows. We could view this gesture literally as giving cows or metaphorically as giving livelihoods to people.

The cow figure that is frequently seen in Krishna shrines across India alludes to his childhood as a cowherd. Small ornamental figures were placed around personal shrines during ritual worship and adorned with flowers and vermilion. This cow figure was cast in the lost wax process with the bell, chain and the forehead ornament die-stamped and chiselled in. The decorative details of the cloth on its back are in the repoussé technique and engraved to show a patterned cloth bordered by a decorative scroll weighed down by pompoms at its four corners. Cows were frequently decorated with vermilion and other colour patterns, and the craftsman alludes to this practice by engraving floral motifs on its body.

Devotional object
Silver
19th century, western India
H-40, W-120, D-77 mm

horse

The horse is not native to India. In fact, the Marwari horse, which comes from the Rajasthan area, is the only Indian breed of the animal. Around 3,500 years ago, the Indo-Aryans arrived in India from the northwest via Kazakhstan, and with them came the horse.

In the Harappan civilisation, which predates the arrival of the Indo-Aryans, there is no sign of the horse. There are no seals that show the horse. The Rig Veda, composed long after the Harrapan cities were destroyed, refers to the horse chariot.

Initially, humans did not ride horses because they were small. They were used to pull chariots instead. The earliest known use of the chariot dates back to around 4,000 years ago, in the area that is now called Kazakhstan. By 1600 BCE, that is around 3,500 years ago, it was also seen in the Anatolia region in modern-day Turkey. The use of horse chariots was also found in Egypt. Warriors like the Hyksos, Hittites and Mittanis used carts pulled by horses instead of mules and donkeys. This means a new draught animal had emerged. The carts, in time, gave way to the chariots.

So, the Indo-Europeans who travelled in the eastern and western directions brought with them a new language and horses. They brought chariots and, importantly, a new technology in the form of the spoked wheel. These are now popular conclusions.

The horse is a very important motif in Hindu art. It is a prized possession. Gods like Indra, Varuna and Ribhus are referred to as using chariots. These gods are mentioned in cuneiform script in Southeastern Turkey and also in Mittani inscription in Anatolia. The sun god is seen as riding a chariot pulled by horses. There is also the famous image of Krishna giving the Bhagavad Gita discourse on a chariot. Ram, too, is visualised on a horse-pulled chariot as he rides out of the city of Ayodhya.

The chariot motif is very important in the Upanishads, too, where it is used as a metaphor. The horse represents the senses, the chariot represents the body and the rider of the chariot represents the soul. In the Puranic period, we have horse-riding men. India was invaded by the Greeks who rode horses, like Alexander. There were the Parthians, the Scythians, the Huns and the Kushans who rode horses. Classical gods like Revanta, the son of the sun god, rode a horse. So while the sun god rides the chariot, his son, who is lord of the chase, rides a horse.

In the case of Buddha, we are told that he is riding through the city in a chariot, when he encounters disease and death. Later, when he leaves the city, he is said to be riding a horse. This marks the transition between the chariot and the horse.

Vishnu's final avatar, Kalki, is also depicted riding a horse. The horse is a symbol of virility and power. When Vishnu takes the form of Hayagriva, he is shown as having the head of a horse.

The horse becomes a very important motif in Hindu traditions, especially with regional gods. Many folk gods are visualised riding horses and holding swords in their hands. They are probably inspired by the numerous Ashwapatis, or master of horses, who came from Northwest India. They include the Indo-Aryans who came on chariots. The Indo-Aryans were followed by the Greeks, who came as horse riders. Then there were the Scythians, also known as Sakas, and the Parthians, the Kushans, the Turks and the Mongols. Finally, a thousand years ago, came the Afghans.

Until the horse came to India, Indian kings were known as Gajapatis, or master of elephants. India would export elephants and import horses. With the arrival of the horse, the kings who controlled the horse trade came to be called as Ashwapatis, and the horse-riding man became a very important motif in temple art as well.

Warrior on a horse
Silver
19th century, western India
H-43, W-55, D-25 mm

This simple figure of a rider atop a horse on its way to battle is cast in silver from a mould. The shield fixed on the rider's back indicates his status as a warrior, holding on to an unidentified weapon over his shoulder. Decorative details etched and carved on the horse are seen prominently on its bridle, saddle, as well as on the rider, his turban and elaborate flared jama. This depth of detail does not progress below the horse's back, down to the legs. The four legs resting on a slender plinth may have been part of a more elaborate ensemble.

dog

The dog is commonly represented in art in India. It is, of course, a loyal animal and we love dogs. However, in traditional Hindu circles, the dog was believed to be inauspicious. The animal is obsessed with its master, who it follows everywhere. It wags its tail when it is happy and whines when the master doesn't feed it well. So, the dog was considered to be a symbol of attachment and ego. Moreover, it was associated with garbage and, therefore, impurity.

In this context, the dog was located opposite to the cow. While the cow was considered auspicious in Hinduism, the dog was believed to be inauspicious. Of course, this is a very broad understanding. Over time, we see the dog gaining significance.

In the Vedas, the mother of dogs is called Sarama, the divine bitch. She produces all the dogs. She goes in search of Indra's cows and finds them and brings them back. So, the role of the dog as a loyal guardian is acknowledged in the Vedas. The mention repeats itself in folk religions in the form of Khandoba and Mallana, both of whom are warrior gods. The dog is also associated with Revanta, the god of the chase. So, you suddenly have the dog appearing as a guardian alongside the one who hunts, the one who goes to war and the one who is a king.

Then, we find the dog linked with Bhairava, the wildest aspect of Shiva that is associated with crematoriums and death. This is an understandable relationship because the dog is associated with death, and with crematoriums and the frontier regions of the society. Bhairava means 'the one who removes the fear of death'.

Bhairava's mildest form is Dattatreya. This form, too, is associated with dogs, but the dogs here are milder. They are considered to be the Vedas, and so there are four of them, for the four Vedas. They always walk in front of Dattatreya, and keep turning around to look at him, insecure and afraid that he will go away.

Therefore, the dog has an ambiguous relationship in Hindu motifs. At one level, it is auspicious in terms of a guardian dog or as the symbol of the followers of Nath traditions—the tantrics, the hermits. On another level, it has a negative connotation where it becomes a symbol of attachment.

Khandoba

Silver

19th century, Deccan Plateau

H-160, W-85, D-60 mm

This silver cast ensemble is made up of three separate components: a rectangular plinth, a dog and a horse on a slender base, and a figure of a man and a woman seated and joined together. The figures fit onto the horse; the mounted horse accompanied by the dog on a base then slides into the rectangular plinth completing the image. The figures are engraved with decorative details to articulate their basic iconography, making them identifiable. Across the Deccan Plateau, a warrior riding a horse with a seated woman on his lap and accompanied by a dog is a depiction of Shiva as Khandoba with Mhalsa as Parvati.

monster

In Greek mythology, a monster is a creature which is a hybrid. It is a mix of different animals. For example, the hero, Bellerophon, confronts the Chimera, which is part-lion, part-goat and part-serpent. He destroys it. But in Hindu mythology, a hybrid creature is considered auspicious. It is seen as a possibility—something that exists not in nature but in the imagination of the gods.

The most common image of this is Narasimha, who is part-lion and part-man. An avatar of Vishnu, Narsimha kills the asura Hiranyakashyapu. So, the idea of monsters is that which exists beyond categories, which merges and unites categories. It represents a space of potential, of possibility.

In the context of monsters or hybrid beings, also known as liminal beings or creatures, the most common motif that we see on the threshold is the Makara, which has the head of an elephant and the tail of a fish. It is the symbol of Capricorn. In Hindu tradition, the elephant is associated with virility or intense sexual energy. It is also associated with water and with power. The fish is always associated with water and thus movement, and so, life. In Western zodiac, Capricorn is represented as part-goat and part-fish. The goat represents virility. It is associated with tenacity, aggressiveness and sexuality in the Western traditions. Therefore, the symbol expresses the same idea as Makara. It is a combination of life, energy, fertility, sexuality and eroticism. Capricorn, sort of, comes around spring—which again is associated with fertility.

The Makara, the elephant-headed fish, is a common motif in Indian art. It is associated with the earrings of Krishna and the banner of Kamadeva, the god of love and lust.

Thus, we see that monsters in Hindu mythology are very different from those in Greek mythology. In Hindu mythology, monsters are not seen as negative things but positive ones.

Sphinx finial

Silver, parcel-gilt

19th century, Deccan Plateau

H-71, W-97, D-45 mm

This unique decorative object, which was originally part of a belted ensemble, shows a sphinx-like figure with the body of a lion, face of a bejewelled woman, wings of a falcon and with bird head talons. The two silver loops at the base would have allowed the object to be anchored on to a belt. The seated figure with its rearing head was mould-cast in silver with further details added by engraving on its turban, neck and wings. Gold plating animates some parts of the figure's head while the hollowed out tubular receptacle attached to the back would have held a plume while in use.

Humans

pots

When an animal is thirsty it goes to the water. Through the invention of pots, humans have managed to get the water to come to them. Pots indicate human creativity: the transformation from animal to human.

In ancient India, before images of gods were worshipped in temples, gods were represented using pots filled with water, grain, gold and auspicious leaves and fruits, like the betel leaf and coconut. The purna-kumbha, or the overflowing pot, represented abundance and fortune.

Lakshmi, the goddess of wealth, holds a pot in her hand. Known as Akshay Patra, or the never-ending pot, it overflows with food constantly. Annapoorna, the kitchen goddess, holds a basket full of food. Vishnu sometimes holds a pot, especially in the form of Dhanvantari, the divine doctor. This pot contains amrita, the nectar of immortality. Brahma holds a pot with a spout, like the one used for religious ceremonies. Balarama and his wife Revati are shown holding a pot filled with wine or Varuni. Shiva being an ascetic is never shown with a pot; he uses a pumpkin shell or a skull to serve as a bowl, to carry food as well to perform ablutions.

During wedding ceremonies, brides kick pots filled with rice into the house to indicate the arrival of fortune. During festivals, pots containing milk and food are placed before images of gods as indicator of prosperity. During funeral ceremonies, pots containing water are ritually broken to indicate the end of life.

In Harappan civilisation, pots were kept next to the dead in the burial grounds. Sometimes bodies were curled and put inside pots. The pots were decorated with sacred motifs like those of peacocks. The pot was seen as a source of life, of food and as a symbol of rebirth, the womb, even then.

Lota/ Kalash
Silver
18th century, south India
H-135, uDia-30, lDia-100 mm

The ubiquitous, bulbous Indian lota with its elongated neck was used to store water for use in religious ceremonies. Engraved within a distinct south Indian decorative idiom, the ten Vishnu avatars depicted are seen within cusped arches and tiered pillars. The elongated neck with smooth, straited engraving allows for an easy grip during handling and is banded at both ends by a simple decorative pattern. A radiating floral petal design further holds the base of the vessel, visually completing it while keeping it stable. The object is a silver response to the traditional Tanjore lota, usually cast in copper or brass with silver additions.

spoons

Although most Indians eat using their fingers and avoid cutlery, the spoon or ladle is an important ritual instrument. It is used to offer clarified butter (ghee) to the gods, during the yagna or homa. It is also used to offer water, milk and fruit juices to the deity during puja. It is called an uddharani, which literally means 'to uplift'.

This draws attention to an important concept in Hindu world view—that of uplifting humanity. Making us rise from our animal instincts to our divine instincts. Animal instincts are rooted in fear and hunger. They make us dominant, territorial and exploitative. But humans can rise above these instincts. We can outgrow fear and hunger, like an ascetic. Or we can focus on other people's fear and hunger and provide them with shelter and nourishment, like an enlightened householder. The spoon represents the latter idea—the ability to feed the other.

While animals grab food, humans have the ability to exchange food. We can give and receive. In the Hindu world view, the noblest being is one who feeds the other without expectation. He trusts the universe to provide for him. He accepts misfortune as part of his fate. He does not blame people. He takes responsibility. He focuses on action, rather than returns. He is a karma-yogi, dedicated to action. He has faith in the cosmos and is hence called a bhakta-yogi. He also understands the complex nature of the impersonal universe, which is why he is also a gyana-yogi. Yogi means one who establishes connection (yoga), of the breath with the body, the body with the mind, the mind with the self, the self with the other.

Ritual spoons are an essential part of yagna and puja. They come in a variety of designs. But the philosophy underlying the object remains about feeding the other. In a compassionate society, humans look out for each other. This is what the spoon represents.

Uddharane/ Ritual Spoon

Silver, enamel

18th century, Rajasthan and south India

H-130, W-26, D-10 mm; H-135, W-30, D-10 mm

Ladling sacred or holy water in temple rituals necessitated the use of ritual spoons. The two similarly shaped spoons here are both cast in silver with details engraved on their surface. Traces of enamel can be seen on the spoon with the speckled stem while the second is more austere in its aesthetic. A triumphant Krishna, playing the flute and dancing over the multi-hooded demon snake Kaliya, completes the finial design, a common feature in such spoons across regions.

footwear

In Buddhist, Jain and Hindu shrines, one finds footprints of a holy man, a god. These are known as Shri-pada (footprint of the goddess of wealth), Vishnu-pada (footprint of Vishnu), Guru-pada (footprint of the guru) or Buddha-pada (footprint of the Buddha). Holy symbols, like the throne, umbrella, flag, yak-tail flywhisk, jewels, fire and a pot of water are seen on the footprint of a holy man or a god. In ancient Buddhist art, Buddha was represented by his footprint. It was only later that an anthropomorphic form was used. We still find such footprints across the Buddhist world.

Along with the footprint, you have the image of the paduka or the footwear. When we talk of footwear, one of the most popular stories is that of Ram. When his stepmother demands that her son, Bharat, should be king of Ayodhya instead of Ram, Ram goes to the forest in exile, without remorse or regret, to clear the path for his younger brother to take the throne. However, Bharat, on learning that the kingdom has been given to him through his mother's political manipulations, rejects it. He goes to Ram, and insists that he return and rule as king. Ram who has given his word to his father that he will live in the forest for fourteen years, can't return just yet. Bharat insists that Ram should symbolically be seen as the king of Ayodhya, while he manages his kingdom, in Ram's absence, as regent. To symbolically represent him, he asks Ram to give his paduka. Ram gives his footwear to Bharat, who brings them to Ayodhya and places them on the royal throne.

A similar story is found in Dashrath Jataka, the Buddhist telling of the Ramayana. There is, however, no mention of Ravan in this tale. Ram-pandita, the eldest son of the king, is told to go to the forest for twelve years because his father fears that his stepmother will kill him. He is told to come back after twelve years when, as per astrologers, Dashrath will be dead and Ram-pandita can rightfully claim the throne. However, while astrology predicts that the father would die after twelve years, he dies earlier, after nine years. Bharat refuses to be king and instead goes to the forest to bring Ram-pandita back. But Ram-pandita insists that he will stay in the forest till the stipulated period of exile is over because that is the word he gave. This integrity of Ram-pandita reveals that he is the Buddha-to-be or the

Bodhisattva. Even here, straw footwear is taken and kept on the throne, till the time of his return three years later.

Humans are the only creatures who wear footwear. So, footwear represents the human potential—our ability to rise above base animal instincts. That is why worship of footwear and footprints of those who have realised their full potential is encouraged in India.

Paduka/ Khadau/ Ritual Footwear
Silver
19th century, western India
H-155, W-72, D-47 mm; H-157, W-70, D-52 mm

Cast silver soles of human feet are stylised and articulated here with the addition of a raised post and knob to be gripped by the big and second toe while walking. The borders of the Paduka are engraved with a decorative scroll and details of birds facing off at the arches. Two circular floral patterns in receding scale are etched onto the feet while a related pattern is engraved on the knob of the footwear's post. Miniature silver paduka were used for ritual worship in honour of a god or a venerated saint in shrines.

ornaments

Animals don't wear ornaments. Humans do. We decorate our body with tattoos, paint our nails and braid our hair; we wear bangles, nose rings and toe rings, necklaces, bracelets and armlets. Harappan cities shown us images of men and women with ornaments. In Hindu temples the gods are adorned with ornaments. The body was thus celebrated—adorned and bedecked.

The Amrapali collection includes ornaments not just for humans but also the gods: tiny anklets, armlets, cummerbunds, necklaces, earrings. The gods loved to be adorned. Mirrors were placed before them so they could enjoy themselves. They had to shimmer in the dark. And jingle as they moved. What could be done had to be overdone.

Hindu and Muslim brides and grooms are adorned with ornaments. It is an indicator of wealth, status and of humanity, the love for beauty, that distinguishes man from beast.

Necklace
Silver gilded
19th century, Cuttack, eastern India
H-940, W-205, D-18 mm

This large silver necklace, meant for a Krishna idol, is made of a central pendant, and floral filigree components that end in a linked chain. The central pendant depicts Krishna playing a flute and a dancing peacock in outline over a dense bed of filigree. The necklace is made of evenly shaped floral blooms in two registers interspersed with rectangular and triangular end pieces that are called tukdi in jewellery parlance. The silver filigree subsequently gilded is a fine example of Tarakashi, a speciality of filigree workers of Cuttack, Orissa, who created myriad objects out of drawn silver wire. Merchants from Shekhawati (Rajasthan) who migrated to eastern India (Bengal, Assam and Orissa) for trade maintained elaborate shrines for their gods. However, this necklace in the north Indian idiom was made using local techniques, creating a unique synthesis of design and aesthetics across two ends of the subcontinent.

hunter

Once civilisation is established there is no real reason to kill animals. Yet, the most common sport of kings is to hunt. The hunter in the forest is a common motif in Indian art. It does not depict the tribal hunter hunting for food, but the king hunting for sport. Typically, the king hunts the deer; occasionally he hunts a tiger or a lion.

The hunt of the deer is a recurring theme in Indian epics. When a king goes hunting for deer, usually disaster looms ahead. In the Ramayana, when Dashrath goes hunting for a deer, he accidentally kills a human being. As a result of this, he is cursed that he will be separated from his son at the time of his death. In the Mahabharata, King Pandu accidentally shoots a hermit who is making love to his wife. Therefore, the hermit curses the king that the latter would die, if he has sexual relations with his wife. In the same epic, the hunting trip of a king called Dushyant leads him to a hermitage. He meets the beautiful Shakuntala and falls in love with her but their story does not end well.

The recurring story of kings pursuing deer is interesting. The word for the deer is 'mriga' and the word for the path is 'marga'. Clearly, there is a co-relation between the wild deer in forests, the hermit who follows the path of the deer, and the king who hunts the deer. It indicates the gradual conquest of nature and the rise of human settlements on cultivated land.

Attardan, Tray and Vase

Silver, gold and blue, green and red glass

19th century, Pratapgarh, western India

Vases: H-168, W-68, D-60 mm;

H-168, W-68, D-61 mm

Tray: H-120, Dia-260 mm

This elaborate tray with an affixed central perfume container, accompanied by two vases, was created using the Thewa technique, a craft speciality of Pratapgarh, Rajasthan. Vignettes of court life, royal hunts, mythological scenes and the circle of life with smaller beings falling prey to larger animals form the central narrative of these objects. In Thewa, fine sheets of silver and gold were delicately punched out to form patterns that were then fused over coloured glass and foiled backs to create small narrative plaques. The concentric circles of the tray with its domed container alongside the multiple registers of the vase are made up of these smaller Thewa plaques in blue, green and red. These were then placed on metal mounts in various shapes to create a suite of souvenirs, popular as presentation items in princely India.

cowherd

With humans appearing on Earth, the world changes completely. What differentiates humans from the animal kingdom is that humans now seek control over nature. They do this to make their lives more comfortable. To bring more certainty into their life, they indulge in practices such as animal husbandry and agriculture. Forests are turned into fields and pastures. In the fields, crops, vegetables and fruit-bearing trees are grown. Orchards are created and gardens are made. In the pastures, sheep, cows and goats graze. Therefore, one of the motifs found in art is the cowherd.

The cowherd is the symbol of a nomadic life. He is the symbol of milk-producing cultures. It is the value placed on getting food from animals without having to kill them. In Vedic thought, the idea of the cowherd is both real and metaphorical.

At the real or literal level, it is an economic activity, providing humans with milk and dung. The milk is food. The dung is fuel and material for building houses. But at the metaphorical level, the cow and the cowherd represent the earth and the king, with the king taking care of the earth, in exchange for the food it gives. The cow motif in Hindu mythology is associated with the earth.

Nagar/ Headpiece
Silver
19th century, south India
H-65, W-55, D-20 mm

Tiny objects with a wealth of decorative detail were the hallmark of master artisans. This headpiece, adapted for use as a pendant, depicts several simultaneous vignettes from young Krishna's life at Vrindavan: his subduing Kaliya, the multi-headed demon snake, him as a flute-playing cowherd and the enactment of his Lila with gopis, his foremost devotees. Figures seen here are created by repoussé and chasing while engraving adds depth of detail, especially in the recesses and borders of the piece. Two rows of large balls tipped by smaller ones are tightly bound to the pendant at its base alluding to bells tinkling. The Nagar was typically placed above the lady's hair plait, which in turn was adorned by a long Jadai. The ensemble together was known as the Jaidainagar.

hermit

The hermit is a recurring motif in art. In fact, it is one of the central themes in Jain art. In Jainism, the hermit is called Shravana, the one who strives to conquer his senses.

A ritual central to Vedic times was the yagna, in which fire played an important role. The yagna was a mediator through which one engaged with the other, and involved trade and exchange between the self and the other.

While yagna is the ritual for churning the fire outside, tapasya is the practice to churn the fire inside. The fire outside is agni; the fire inside, tapa. It is on tapa that the hermit focuses. This occurs as the austerities of the hermit, the mendicant and the yogi. He shuts his eyes to the external world and withdraws to the inner world. He churns the spiritual fire of tapa. Using this fire, he explores the inner world of sensations, emotions, thoughts, dreams, memories and imagination. In the process, he breaks all attachment to the outside world by understanding its truth. The fire, tapa, is a metaphor for the light that reveals wisdom and helps us see the world as it is. It is the heat that gives us the strength to break our attachment to delusions. Therefore, the word 'tapasvi' is used in Hinduism. While in Jainism, the words used are shravana, muni, sadhaka, or the one who strives, and arhat. Another word used is yogi.

With the arrival of the hermit, Indian philosophy changes dramatically. There is tension between the external world and the internal world. The external world is informed by those who explore the inner world. The rishi explores the outer world, while the tapasvi explores the inner world. The value placed on the world of feelings, sensations, emotions, desires and wants is the greatest contribution of India to the entire external world. Human insecurities and hunger, which make us possessive, jealous, ambitious, aggressive and greedy, are not a part of the hermit. The hermit is the Mahavir.

Mahavir is to be contrasted with the vir, or the hero, or the brave one, who defeats threats from the outside. The vir is the guardian of the city, the protector of the village. He is the great hero who defeats the villain. The mahavir conquers the restless, insecure and nervous mind which constantly seeks validation from the external world. This conversation between the vir and the mahavir, the hero and the hermit, is the dominant theme of Indian philosophy. This is similar to the tension between the wild forest and the domesticated field, and between the wild forest fire and the domesticated kitchen fire.

In Hinduism, there is tension between the hermit and the householder. There is constant conflict between their respective worlds. The hermit is a common feature in all mythology. He is the rishi, the tapasvi, the yogi. We constantly wonder which path to take. In ancient times, once the student completed his education, he had three choices. He could become a householder, a rishi or a hermit. Each had different modalities.

A rishi is somewhere between the hermit and the householder. He is a householder who does not have property. He lives in the forest. He only has one cow in his possession. He lives off the forest almost like a hunter-gatherer. He depends upon the king for his livelihood but he does get married and have children. He is called a Vanaprasthi or the forest dweller. The hermit, a celibate monk, on the other hand, possesses nothing. He does not marry. He has no family. He does not stay in a single place for more than a night, and takes refuge in caves, during the rainy season.

So, a person could choose to be a householder, a forest dweller or a wandering mendicant. Later, in the classical Hindu period we are told these are sequential choices. So, you begin your life as a student, become a householder and then become a forest dweller. Going to dwell in the forest means that you retire from the household world. You pass on your property and your knowledge to the next generation. Having done so, the forest dweller, after the death of his spouse, becomes a wandering hermit. He accepts death and completely detaches himself from the material world. Thus, we see the social structure of the Vedic society aligns with the spiritual battles that are going on between the inner world and the outer world.

Parshvanath Gatta Ji/ Portable Jain Shrine
Silver, gold, glass
20th century, Pratapgarh, western India
H-58, W-50, D-10 mm

The Thewa technique in Pratapgarh, Rajasthan, was frequently used to make small portable personal shrines for adherents of Jainism. Here, fine sheets of gold are cut in profile with delicate patterns punched out and fused over green glass, creating an image of Parshvanath in outline. The piece is further backed with gold foil to add depth and luminosity to the figure and sealed within a silver case. A cover over the case protects the image during travel. A blooming flower over the cover is etched by repoussé and chasing while a ring of fine granulation completes the sparse design. A round loop at the tip of the flower is used as a knob to open the case.

couples in art

One of the common Hindu motifs is that of a man and woman holding each other intimately. This image is found in Buddhist and Jain shrines, too. This is the image of the Dampatya, also known as the Mithun image.

At one level, such images represent the foundational relationship of human society, between man and woman, which creates the family. At another level, it is a metaphor, with the man representing the spiritual aspect and the woman representing the material aspect of life. In the Mahabharata, in Sankhya philosophy, the male or spiritual aspect of life is known as 'purusha', while the female or material aspect of life is known as 'prakruti'. Later, the male aspect is called Pingla and the female aspect is called Ida.

Some say it is similar to the Chinese yin and yang, with a slight difference. Chinese yin and yang are both located in the material plane. Therefore, Ida and Pingla usually align with the concept of yin and yang, with Ida being yin and Pingla being yang, the cold and hot aspects or the lunar and solar aspects of material life. But when we use the words purusha and prakruti, there is a difference. Purusha refers to the spiritual or psychological aspect of existence: the emotions, intellect, memory and sensations, which can't be measured. What one can measure is the physical manifestation of it. The physical manifestation is called prakruti, the goddess or the female.

Many people ask why the female form is associated with the material world and the male form with the psychological or spiritual world, and not the other way round. The answer comes from two standpoints: one, in an inherently patriarchal society, men are seen as superior to women. Therefore, when you associate men with the spirit and mind, it means that the spirit and mind are superior to the body. This is how most celibate gurus talk. The spirit is always positioned above the body. In Buddhism and Jainism, the hermit is seen as being superior to the householder. The married couple embodies the householder, and rejection of the female is seen as the higher path. This obviously is not solely a spiritual approach. There exist, in the hermit traditions of India, patriarchal foundations.

The second standpoint comes from a non-patriarchal level. The female form lends itself to symbolically represent the material because life is created within a woman's body. A child is created inside a woman's body and outside a man's body. So, the female form lends itself to represent material reality. The male form lends itself to the non-material, which can be termed as the psychological or spiritual reality.

This miniature plaque depicts a married couple and was possibly used as part of a family shrine representing deceased forbears. An arch-shaped gold sheet is chiselled and raised with distinct modelling to create the human figures with added motifs. The torana-like arch is similarly detailed with graded circular patterns emerging from terminals shaped like mythical beasts. It is affixed to a silver back and pedestal which shows reinforcement over the ages, a testimony to the place of significance it held in the family's memory.

Plaque
Gold, silver
19th century, Deccan Plateau
H-62, W-42, D-30 mm

Goddess

ganga

Ganga is the most sacred river in India. According to the Puranas, it used to flow in the heavens, in Swarga Loka. The kings of the solar dynasty, the Suryavamshis, brought it down to Earth. The Ramayana tells this story of how Bhagiratha, from the solar dynasty, invoked the gods. He asked them to send Ganga from the heavens to earth. He asked this to give his forefathers a chance at a second life. The fall of Ganga could split the earth, and, to prevent this, Shiva's help was sought. Shiva captured the falling Ganga in his matted locks and enabled the river to flow gently down to the sea.

This story is central to Hindu belief as it connects the earth to the heavens. It is also important because it brings both Shiva and Vishnu into the story. Ganga was created when the heavenly waters were used to wash the feet of Vishnu. Therefore, she is called Vishnupadi. So, she falls from the feet of Vishnu onto the head of Shiva, before falling onto earth. This multistage journey establishes the river's sacredness. In art, the river-goddess is visualised as a woman holding a pot riding a river dolphin, or makara.

Ganga now flows on Earth, enabling humans to be reborn. When we die and our ashes are cast into the Ganga, rebirth will happen. If our ashes are not thrown into the Ganga, rebirth will not happen. Rebirth is the cornerstone of Hindu, Jain and Buddhist philosophy. This idea probably originated in the Gangetic plains, which is why the Ganga gets such a great value.

In the Vedas, there is reference to another river called the Sindhu. The Sindhu is River Indus. In the Vedas, the concept of rebirth is not defined. The idea, however, consolidates and becomes a part of Hindu tradition by the time the Vedas give way to the Puranas. The intellectual journey from the Vedas to the Puranas is mapped by the geographical journey of the Aryans. They travel from the Indus valley, currently in Pakistan, to the Gangetic plains, in the eastern part of north India. This journey, over a thousand years, from 1500 BCE to 500 CE, marks a shift in Indian thought, with the consolidation of the idea of rebirth. Therefore, Ganga plays a very important role in the idea of rebirth.

Over time, the word 'Sindhu', which meant Indus, came to represent all rivers. Thus, India is called Sapta-sindhu-sthala, the land of seven rivers. Originally, it meant the Indus valley and its tributaries. Later, it represents the seven great rivers of India, including Ganga, Yamuna, Krishna, Kaveri, Godavari and Narmada. All rivers were then associated with rebirth and Ganga. So, the southern rivers are call Dakshina Ganga.

The concept of Ganga as a river which gives birth to life is related to its fertile riverbanks that bring agricultural potential. This was not unique to India. Every civilisation in the world thrived on the banks of a river. It happened in China, with River Yellow; in Mesopotamia, with the Tigris and Euphrates rivers; and in Egypt, with the Nile.

What is unique about the Ganga is the spiritual meaning it holds. The river makes us recognise that we live infinite lives, that this life of ours is one of many lives. The idea extends across India, especially in the city of Kashi or Banaras, where the river takes a northern turn. According to beliefs, the north-to-south flow of a river represents our journey from life to death. When a river reverses its direction, moving from south to north, it represents a spiritual possibility that is against the order of nature. It then represents the idea that we can break away from the cycle of rebirth and attain moksha.

This water pot, popularly called the Gangajali, is an elaborate container to store the sacred water of the Ganges. Extensive use of repoussé and chasing techniques, besides chiselling in of details, articulates Shiva and Shaivite symbols. Figures within cusped arches are seen across the widest extremity of the gilded pot and would have needed great skill in execution, especially across a curved surface. Stylised floral and vegetal patterns are seen on the rest of the body of the pot. The lid that screws on to the neck has a sculpted face of the Goddess Ganga as a finial. Across the subcontinent, similar pots were used to store the water from the holy Ganges for religious and death rituals.

Gangajali/ Pot
for Ganges Water
Silver, parcel-gilt
19th century, north India
H-142, W-110, lDia-54 mm

godavari

The period after 500 BCE witnessed the spread of Buddhism and Jainism beyond the Gangetic plains. Likewise, the Brahmins, too, spread Vedic and Puranic ideas when they travelled to various parts of India. Wherever they travelled, they took the idea of Ganga with them. So, across India, all other rivers were called Dakshina Ganga and all the mountains were considered to be Dakshina Kailasa.

One such river is Godavari, which flows in the central part of India. It moves from the west to the east, and it is a rain-fed river. Since Godavari is not snow-fed, it is not perennial. Because of this, it is not considered to have descended from the heavens or Swarga, the realm of the immortal gods.

However, the Godavari is still considered sacred. The story goes that Goddess Parvati came to be annoyed that Ganga always sat on her husband's, Shiva's, head. To get rid of her, she seeks help from her son, Ganesha. Taking the form of a cow, Ganesha goes south to the hermitage of a sage named Gautama. Gautama tries to shoo the cow away from his crops and strikes her with a stalk of rice. Ganesha, the cow, pretends to die instantly. Realising that he has committed the grave crime of killing a cow, Gautama invokes the gods for a way to cleanse himself from this sin. Ganesha then appears before Gautama and tells him to pray to Shiva and request him to send Ganga to the south. That is how Ganga leaves her home in the Himalayas, descending from the head of Shiva, and comes to the south as Godavari.

Plaque
Silver, copper
19th century, central India
H-81, W-98, D-9 mm

This plaque, a religious souvenir possibly acquired at a pilgrimage site, depicts a tiered registry of the major gods of the Hindu pantheon with Shiva at its centre. Silver sheet undergoes extensive and minute repoussé and chasing to indicate brief outlines filled in with recognisable iconographic details of the gods depicted. Their names have similarly been etched above each figure. To the left of the central figure of Shiva is Goddess Godavari with four hands. She is holding floral blooms, a flower garland and a water pot. The plaque is further backed with lac resin to retain its shape and details, ending with a copper sheet cover and a silver loop to aid display.

पार्वती
गोदावरी
वणीची देवी
कृष्णा

लक्ष्मी
दत्तात्रेय
विष्णु

lakshmi

Lakshmi is the goddess of wealth and fortune. She is visualised as seated on a lotus flower. She also holds lotus flowers in her hands and a pot overflowing with grain and gold.

Goddess Lakshmi is worshipped not only in Hinduism but also in Buddhism and Jainism. In fact, the earliest images of Lakshmi are found on Buddhist stupas. Later, we find them in Jain scriptures, as appearing in the dreams of the mothers of holy men. In Hindu art, we find them in the coins of the Gupta kings, who were patrons of Hinduism. In Hindu art, Lakshmi is distinguished by being visualised with four arms, not two.

Goddess Lakshmi is considered to be whimsical. She comes and goes as she pleases. Everybody wants her—from the devas to the asuras, to the yakshas and the nagas. Everybody tries to grab her. But Vishnu is the only deity who is able to attract her by doing dharma. While everyone focuses on their own hunger, success and desire for glory, Vishnu seeks to enable others to find food, glory and fame. Thus, by helping others, he makes himself a magnet for the goddess of wealth.

Lakshmi
Silver
20th century, western India
H-220, W-160, D-60 mm

The figure of the goddess seated on a platform shaped like a lotus bloom was beaten and carved over a wooden central core. The figure of the goddess is sparingly engraved and etched to show details of her clothing and of the lotus blooms in her hands. The etched plinth shows distinct lotus petals traditionally associated as her seat. This sculpture is part of a larger group of fourteen similarly detailed objects that represent the fourteen dreams that Mahavira's mother Trishala had before his birth. Her fourth dream was of Lakshmi, the goddess of wealth and prosperity, and hence its depiction.

saraswati

Saraswati is the goddess of knowledge. She is visualised as dressed in white, holding a Veena, or a lute, or an Ektara, in one hand and memory beads in the other. She rides a goose or a hansa. The goose is a special animal. In Indian mythology, it is believed to have the ability to separate milk from water. Thus, it is the symbol of analytical skills, which are necessary for knowledge.

The goddess is said to be distant and aloof. She doesn't care for anyone. It is very difficult to get her; but once she comes into your life, she doesn't leave you. This is in contrast to her sister, Lakshmi, the goddess of fortune, who comes and goes as she pleases. When one dies, one leaves one's wealth behind, but not one's knowledge. All we can leave behind is a bunch of information, recorded in texts.

Goddess Laxmi is considered the consort of Vishnu. Goddess Saraswati is considered the consort of Brahma. These ideas emerged in Puranic times. They bring a sense of symmetry, by seeing each god having a goddess. Saraswati, however, is visualised independently. The word 'Saraswati' comes from the sound 'sarasa', which means the trembling of water. So, water bodies are associated with Saraswati. The word 'sarovar' means a lake; the word 'sarita' means a river.

Saraswati has many forms. At one level, she is the patron of the arts, music, painting and dance. All artists worship her. She is also the goddess of skills. Skills that help us generate wealth and power. Skills that help us establish society and govern. She, thus, helps to establish the practical side of life. Finally, the third and the most subtle and sublime form of Saraswati is that which enables spiritual growth. This is done via self-reflection and the understanding of our bodies. Ultimately, she helps us in realising the true nature of the self.

Inkwell
Silver
19th century, Rajasthan
H-81, W-78, D-78 mm

Saraswati, the goddess of learning, features on the front of this four-sided inkwell. The other three sides feature Ganesha, Devi and Krishna with Radha, all framed within cusped arch-shaped shrines. Silver was hammered, bent and soldered to form the rigid frame of the box. Images of the gods were then delicately chased, etched and engraved on its surface. The attached moveable circular lid depicting the sun god was made using repoussé and chasing techniques. That the artisan had refined skill is evident in the use of simple etching tools to depict complex figures with detailed iconographies.

durga

One of the most important goddesses in Hindu mythology is Durga. The goddess is shown with many arms, holding many weapons in her hands. Sometimes, she is depicted as having four arms, sometimes eight and sometimes even ten. She rides a lion or a tiger. Durga exists between the world of the hermit and the householder. She stands between the wild and the domestic world.

She is untamed. She cannot be controlled, ordered or instructed. This is represented by the fact that she rides a tiger, which is a wild animal. However, Durga is also a part of the domesticated world. In her hand, she holds the weapons to defend territory, or the property of humanity. She is the goddess of the fortress, or fence. Hence the name Durga, which comes from the word 'durg', meaning fortress. She is the goddess of kings. She is located outside citadels. She protects the citadels from the wild forces of nature. At the same time, she is too wild to be contained.

She is not the housewife; she is the warrior goddess. The warrior goddess is believed to be a part of village folklore. She became part of mainstream society, when the Kushans ruled in India, nearly 2,000 years ago. Across the Middle East, we find the concept of the goddess of love and war, Ishtar. Ishtar rides lions and the same idea comes to India in the form of Durga. She is the goddess who domesticates Shiva. She domesticates herself to become Gauri. She is a liminal being, located between the wild Kali, the forest, and the domesticated Gauri, the field.

The classic story of Durga is the one wherein she defeats Mahishasura. The tiger-riding goddess defeats the buffalo demon. What is interesting to note here is that the asura, or demon, is associated with a domesticated animal, the buffalo, while the guardian is associated with a wild animal, the tiger. This irony reflects the tension between the forest-dwelling tribes, the vanaprasthis, and the gruhasthis, the one who cultivated the land, created the villages and turned the forests into fields and pastures. The goddess thus reminds us of the continuous tension between the domesticated and the wild world. The tension between the buffalo and the tiger. Sometimes, the tiger wins.

Plaque
Silver
20th century, Karnataka
H-672, W-235, D-60 mm

Shrines across India have a tradition where idols are often covered with silver plaques donated as votive offerings by devotees. This large Durga plaque in her form as Mahishasura Mardini shows her slaying the buffalo demon. Of her four hands, the lower two, which are now incomplete, would have held the spear to assail the buffalo with. While repoussé and chasing techniques were used to great effect to model her figure and show details of her costume and jewellery, it is the large unadorned sections that add visual potency and vigour to the figure.

saptamatrika

One of the most common motifs that you find in Hindu art is the image of the seven women, the Saptamatrika. These seven women are always seen as a group, as a collective. We have found these images in the Harappan civilisation, too. This means they go back to pre-Vedic times, over 4,000 years ago. There are references to this group of seven in the Vedas. It is a consistent theme, found not only in India but also around the world. In all probability, it refers to the Pleiades constellation or the Kritika constellation. They are also referred to as the seven sisters of the forest; wild, untamed, mysterious beings linked to forests and rivers, who are worshipped in times of crisis.

In folk religions, these women are considered to be independent, autonomous women, who live in the forest. They are associated as wild beings. They are both malevolent as well as benevolent, which means they have a negative side as well as a positive one. If they are not appeased, they can make women infertile, or cause them to have a miscarriage, or give birth to a malformed baby or be beset by diseases like measles. Therefore, these goddesses are typically venerated by women during pregnancy, when the baby is small, and when the child falls ill.

This collective of goddesses is known variously as yoginis, dakinis, matrikas and kritikas. In Shaivite mythology, they are the nursemaids of Shiva's son, Kartikeya. The name 'Kartikeya' comes from 'the one who was given milk by the kritikas'. These women are mothers, but they don't have husbands. They received the power to kill unborn and newborn infants, if they were not venerated by mothers. This malevolent form was later made benevolent as they were seen as wet nurses who care for unborn and newborn children.

In Brahmana literature, the Saptarishis, the seven great sages, identified with the Big Dipper constellation, had seven wives. They accused at least six of their wives of infidelity. The women argued that they were innocent. Extremely upset at being wrongly accused, they moved away from the Saptarishi constellation to form the Kritika constellation on their own. So, in a way, there is a lot of gender tension between the Saptamatrikas and the Saptarishis.

The seven-sister collective is a protective talisman. It is associated with fertility, maternity and the wild forest. These are not domesticated goddesses. You rarely find them in temples. They may be found on the exterior walls of temples, but mostly these are goddesses of folklore.

Saptamatrika
Silver
18th century, north India
H-52, W-107, D-20 mm

The Saptamatrikas or the seven goddesses worshipped as folk deities are usually forged in iron or carved in stone and wood. The lack of precise iconography for the seven mothers has meant that here they are cast in silver as generic female figures with barely modelled faces or limbs. Their hair has been teased into coils and they hold on to an indeterminate post while being anchored onto a narrow plinth. The figure would have been part of a larger shrine.

Gods

brahma

Brahma is the creator. He is, however, the creator of life, not the world. In Hindu traditions, the world is eternal, but life comes and goes. Life's appearance is attributed to Brahma. In this, he must be differentiated from God of biblical traditions, or Allah of Islamic tradition, who are identified as 'creator'.

God/Allah is an all-powerful creator of the world as well as of life; he gives laws via messengers on how humans should live; he determines their fate after death. This is monotheistic mythology. But in Hindu mythology, Brahma is one aspect of the divine. He embodies life—the ability to sense the world around and respond to it, and the hunger and the fears that drive us to engage with the world. He needs to be complemented with Vishnu and Shiva, and with the goddesses, who embody other aspects of life. Brahma is not located outside the world, in heaven. Like Shiva and Vishnu, he, too, is located within all living creatures. Which is why, in Indian art, it is common to show images of a human form containing all the worlds, including the realms of the gods.

Brahma, in the Upanishads, is said to have been the first sentient being. He was the first to became aware of himself and experience loneliness. Because he experienced loneliness, he created other creatures. So, other creatures exist to take away our loneliness. Brahma, as the creator of life, naturally becomes the creator of hunger and fear. Shiva, the great ascetic, who destroys hunger and fear, becomes the destroyer. So, Brahma is not the creator of world. He is the creator of life, hunger and fear. Shiva is not the destroyer of the world. He is the destroyer of the living condition. He enables you to outgrow hunger and fear. So, Brahma and Shiva are always at loggerheads. A balance is achieved between them through Vishnu. Vishnu focuses on the idea of outgrowing personal hunger while satisfying the hunger of others. Thus, he balances the two schools of thought.

In the Puranas, Brahma is visualised as an old priest with four heads, who has implements for a yagna in his hand. The four heads represent the four Vedas, the four shastras, four different ways of looking at the world, that often do not see eye-to-eye. Yagna is the ritual by which relationships are

Umlaka/ Mukut/ Crown
Silver
19th century, Himachal Pradesh, north India
H-451, W-302, D-16 mm

established with the other. The ritual establishes exchange. It is the ritual that creates human society. Brahma establishes this yagna. He also creates the various beings who take part in it.

Through his sons and grandsons, who marry various female beings, Brahma creates life. This makes him the ultimate fountainhead of plants, animals, birds, fishes and reptiles. He creates the hoarders known as yakshas, the grabbers known as rakshasas and the hungry spirits known as the pretas. Some of his descendants are known as devas and they live in the celestial regions; others live under the earth as nagas and asuras. Brahma is the common grandfather of all living creatures. This is why Hindus believe that the whole world is one family, giving rise to the Sanskrit phrase 'vasudhaiva kutumbakam'. We have a common ancestor in Brahma and the world, or Earth, is our inheritance. Unfortunately, the children of Brahma fight over this inheritance, each one claiming what they feel is their fair share.

Once, the devas, the asuras and humans went to Brahma and asked how they can be happy. Brahma said to the devas, who loved indulgence, to restrain their desires. To the asuras, who loved to frighten and control people, he said to try being kind. To humans, who were eternally insecure, he said try being generous. Thus, Brahma acknowledges the diversity of life—no single solution for all problems, no one set of rules for all beings.

A variety of silver smithy techniques were used to create this elaborate three-panelled turban ornament. Brahma, the creator of life with four heads and hands, is not often represented in jewellery or religious structures. Here he marks his presence with Vishnu and Shiva, the other two members of the holy trinity. They are unusually accompanied by the figure of Devi, the goddess. Silver was soldered and hammered, bent, stamped and further shaped into forms for designs to be realised using repoussé and chasing techniques. Linked chains were subsequently attached to create a fringe and help anchor the piece on the turban. Across Himachal Pradesh and other northern regions, such crowns were tied to a bridegroom's turban, invoking gods to sanctify the union and protect the groom from malevolent beings.

shiva

Shiva is easily recognised as the god who holds a trident, wears animal hide, has a snake around his neck and a top knot from which water spouts. He is one of three main gods of Hinduism. A popular and powerful god, he is linked to destruction—not destruction of the world, but destruction of desires, which in turn destroys death, and grants liberation from the cycle of rebirths.

The story of Shiva is the journey of the hermit to the householder. While the Jain and Buddhist traditions focused on kings who became hermits, the Shiva tales of Hindus speak of the reverse: a hermit who becomes a householder. In Jain and Buddhists traditions, a king gives up his kingdom, his queen, his children, his property, wealth, horses and elephants. He even gives up the clothes on his body and the hair on his head. He then becomes a hermit. After he gives up all he possesses, he becomes known as a Digambara, the one who has abandoned all property. The literal meaning of Digambara is one who is sky-clad. He is the wandering, naked ascetic who possesses nothing. He has no relationships and has completely detached himself from the material world. However, in the Shiva stories, we find the Digambara becoming a Grahasti. The story of a wandering ascetic who possesses nothing and is forced to become part of a household by the goddess Shakti.

If Brahma is linked to yagna, or the ritual of exchange, Shiva is linked to tapasya, the practice of meditation and contemplation that destroys all hungers and fears, and helps one outgrow dependence on the external world. He, therefore, lives in the crematorium, where life ends, and in stony, icy mountains where no life grows. He is comfortable with desolation and prefers solitude. But everyone wants him to engage with life and share his wisdom and skills with the world. Hence stories of his marriage and the creation of his two sons form the foundation of his lore.

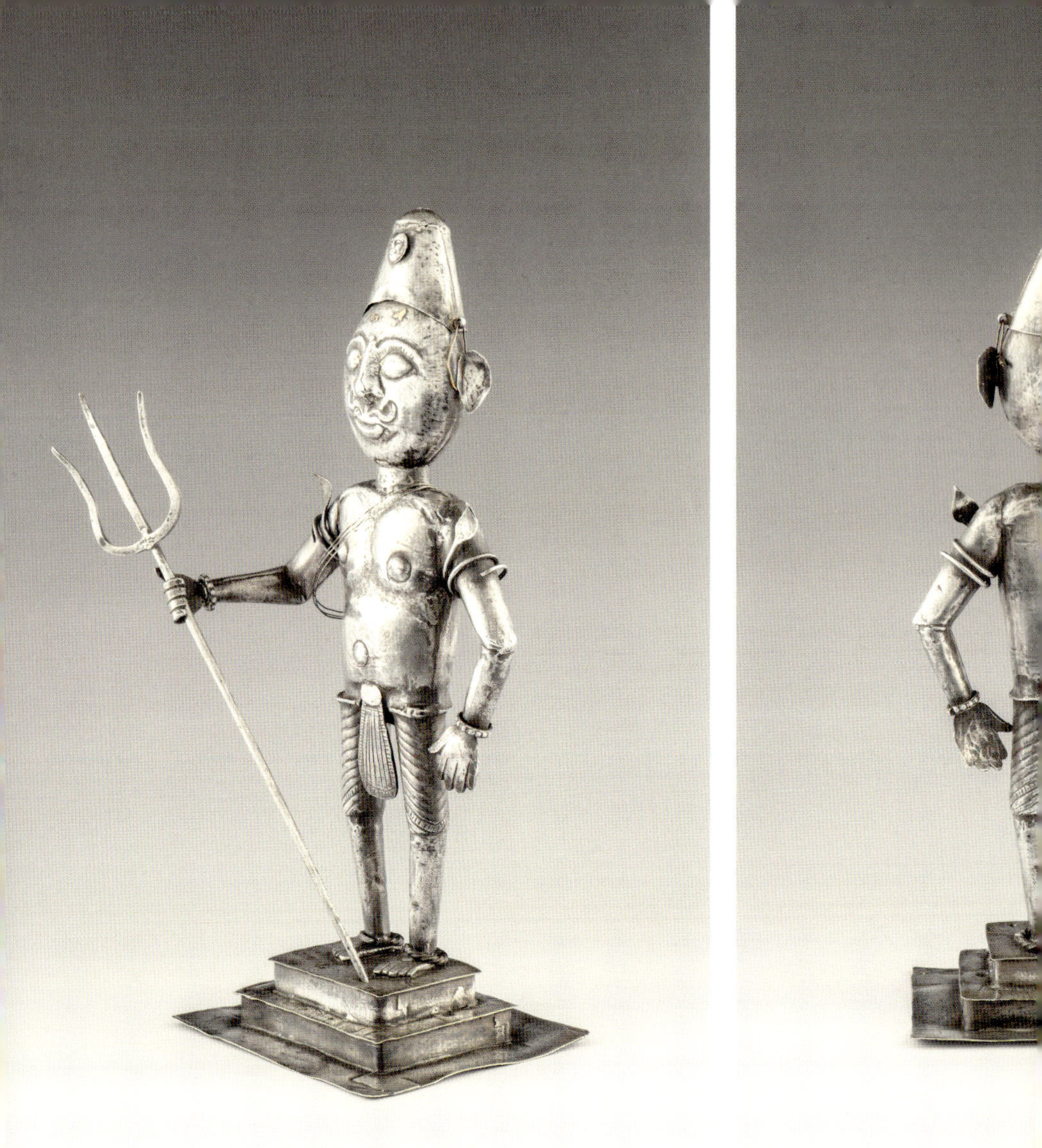

Shiva
Silver
19th century, Deccan Plateau
H-288, W-190, D-103 mm

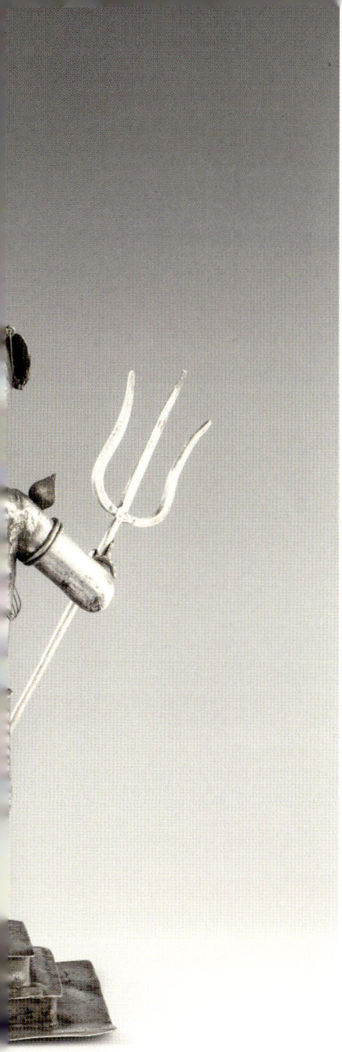

Tribal forms of sculpture don't adhere to classical proportions in their imagery. They, however, create figures of raw emotive energy that leave great impact on the viewer. Shiva as seen here is created from silver sheets that were hammered, bent and soldered to create the essential form with iconographic details engraved and accoutrements added. Shiva's prominent forehead with his third eye and other parts of his face show past traces of gilding. The goddess Ganges is perched on his conical hat anchored to his ears, a departure from traditional depictions of matted hair. Silver serpents are wound as armbands and a sacred thread is rigidly coiled around his torso.

mukhalingam

Some of the peculiar objects that one finds in the Amrapali Jewels Museum collection are masks that are placed on the Shivalinga. This draws attention to the Shivalinga, which is a popular object of worship in Hinduism.

Western scholars often describe the Shivalinga as a phallic symbol. Such a description upsets Hindus, as it is akin to referring to the crucifix as a torture instrument, or the Qabah as a room.

This description has a strategic purpose behind it. European scholars wanted to establish India's status as pagan in the 19th century, to facilitate religious conversion. This was carried forward by 20th-century American academicians, who high-handedly dismissed the devotee's view as denial.

The word 'linga' means attribute. Shivalinga means the attribute of the one without attributes, the form of the formless. It is the symbol of that which cannot be symbolised—the atma, the spirit that grants us life, makes us sentient, but is itself beyond birth and death.

It is said that Shiva first appeared as a pillar of fire that had no foundation or tip. It had no beginning or end. It anchored all existence. The gods decided to worship Shiva as a pillar, or a rounded stone (known as pinda) either rising from the earth or fixed into earth.

A Shivalinga is a stone that is found in a river, polished by the river's flowing waters. In other words, its very shape is organic. It is not created by man. It is an image that is self-created. Hence, called Svayambhu. This stone polished by the river is then placed in a trough. The trough represents the goddess, nature, who anchors the spirit and makes it accessible. To make it even more accessible, it is given a mask of a human face (mukha). This makes it the mukhalinga. If nothingness is zero or shunya and the possibilities of infinity exist, the face represents the space between zero and infinity.

Thus, the Shivalinga, with its mukhalinga, is trying to explain the abstract idea of the creation in Hinduism. A creation in which divinity has infinite potential. It gradually manifests itself from the formless to form.

Face masks are often placed in front of a Shivalinga to create an iconic form over the aniconic. Frequently damaged amidst daily wear and tear during rituals, they were replaced regularly with fresh votive offerings from devotees. Solid silver sheets were beaten into shape and soldered and hammered into place to create this visual representation of Shiva, the serpent seen coiled around his neck and hair. While basic iconography was adhered to, local styles would take precedence in the creating of mukhalingas. Here, for instance, bushy eyebrows and moustache in black enamel with traces of other colours add individuality to the figure.

Mukhalingam
Silver, enamel
20th century, Deccan Plateau
H-240, W-100, D-50 mm

shiva-shakti

As Hindus chose to use stories to communicate abstract ideas, the atma or spirit was visualised as male and nature or substance was visualised as female. Shiva was the male. Shakti was the female.

Shiva is the great hermit who sits atop a snow-covered stone mountain. Through the practice of tapasya he draws in all heat into his body, leaving the world around him cold and desolate, with no flora or fauna. He embodies the wisdom of the hermit. But what use is this wisdom, if it does not help society?

So, Shakti comes into his life. She draws the knowledge out of him and brings it back to society. In other words, she causes the snow to melt and transforms it into a river that nurtures society. She is the soil in which the seed of wisdom germinates. Shiva is the seed. Thus, the union of Shiva and Shakti—the primal man and the primal woman—is the transformation of wisdom into a very practical, worldly form.

Jainism and Buddhism talk about the journey of the disillusioned, unenlightened householder to becoming the enlightened hermit. The story of Shiva and Shakti speaks about the transformation of the enlightened hermit into the enlightened householder. He engages with the world and brings his knowledge to Earth, with her help. Thus, there are images of Shiva and Shakti together. The goddess questions him. She forces the silent Shiva to speak and share his understanding of the world through stories.

The stories reveal the Hindu world, which is without beginning and end and which goes through endless transformation. There are stories of rebirth, of how society rises and falls. Stories of the struggle between the inner world and outer world, and of the conflict between material and spiritual things. Stories of the desire to create order. Stories about the inability to control the human mind. Stories about the quest of humans to control fire, water, plants and animals.

All these are a part of Shiva's conversation with Shakti. They become so close to each other that they merge. There is no separation between the observer and the observed, the teacher and the student. Therefore, Shiva and Parvati become halves of each other's body. This form of Shiva is known as Ardhanareshwar, half-man and half-woman.

Some people look at it as a simple sexual a-gendering quality. Others see it as a union of the material and spiritual where the material world telescopes into the spiritual world and vice versa. This seems that the study of the body takes us to the mind and the study of the mind takes us to the study of the body. The study of the self takes us towards society and the study of society takes us to the self. It shows the coming together of opposite and complementary ideas. It can be seen as the female form representing the word and the male form representing meaning. Meaning has no form and depends on the word to manifest itself. Therefore, the manifested word represents the goddess, Shakti. The unmanifested meaning represents the god, Shiva.

The simplicity and great clarity of thought in design is what makes this pendant unique. The base plate is partitioned in two registers with the upper half depicting Parvati attending on Shiva within a domestic setting. The lower portion captures their respective vahanas or mounts, the tiger and Nandi the bull, seated in quiet repose. Created for a Shiva-Shakti adherent, the central figures are delineated using the repoussé and chasing techniques with details chiselled and soldered on. The borders and the central line are die-stamped.

Pendant
Silver
19th century, north India
H-74, W-73, D-11 mm

virabhadra

There are many stories about the marriage of Shiva and Shakti. One of them involves the Brahmin patriarch, Daksha. Daksha's youngest daughter, Sati, chooses to marry the wandering ascetic, Shiva. It is a marriage not appreciated by the father, who tries to control his daughter. Daksha is so angry with Sati's display of independence that he rejects his daughter.

Daksha conducts a great yagna ceremony. Everyone is invited, except Shiva, his son-in-law, who is chosen by his daughter of her own free will. In rejecting Shiva, he is rejecting the daughter who has displayed independence. He has also rejected the god who does not align with the exchange paradigm of the yagna. A god who lives on his own terms and who prefers the hermit ways, the ascetic ways to the householder ways. One who prefers the isolation and solitude of mountains. One who prefers the inner world over the outer world. One who chooses to be with his thoughts, feelings and ideas. One who has rejected the world of relationships, property, wealth, power and knowledge. This tension manifests into great conflict. It reaches the point where Sati, enraged when she fails to reconcile her husband with her father, jumps into the fire pit and burns herself to death. This causes a clash between her husband and her father.

This is when Shiva, the detached hermit, transforms into a fierce warrior. In this form he is called Virabhadra, whose image is found in Indian art. The name Virabhadra indicates his righteous outrage, at the treatment of his wife, Sati, by her father, Daksha. He raises his sword and destroys the yagnashala.

The foundational Vedic ritual, the yagna, is destroyed by Shiva. This indicates a violent clash between the old, Vedic tradition and the indigenous tradition, which focuses on the inner world rather than the outer world. This is a world of tapa, of contemplation over the world of exchange, trade and relationships. A great battle takes place and Daksha is beheaded. But then the gods beg Shiva to reconsider and reconcile with the opposing parties. So, Daksha is brought back to life with a goat's head. The yagna is restored.

The purpose of ritual is to engage with people, not to disassociate from them. Daksha uses his yagna to distance himself from his daughter and his son-in-law. By doing so, he goes against the very essence of the yagna, which is to bring people together through exchange.

Plaque
Silver, copper
19th century, Karnataka/ Maharashtra
H-195, W-154, D-55 mm

Karnataka's unique tradition of Virabhadra devotion is credited with a robust tradition of devotional plaques crafted with great ingenuity. A solid silver sheet is hammered and raised to create the iconographic form, which is then modelled and detailed by engraving and chiselling. Backed with lac to seal and protect it from the inside, it is further strengthened by metal backing, here copper. This minutely detailed plaque shows Shiva as Virabhadra, a four-armed figure depicted in local folk idiom holding a bow and an arrow, a trident, and a shield under a makara torana crowned by a Kirtimukha. A Shivalinga and Nandi the bull flank the central figure from the upper extremities, completing all essential aspects of depiction.

shiva family

In Hindu temples, god is represented as a family. The most common representation is of Shiva, with his wife, Shakti, and their two sons, Ganesha and Kartikeya. This is a metaphor for worldly life. Shiva, the hermit, is transformed into Shankara, the householder.

Shiva now had to solve household issues. All household issues, in Hinduism, are classified into two groups. The first is the yearning for food to nourish our bodies. Therefore, the yearning for prosperity, wealth, power and success. The second is the yearning for security and peace. We want to be secure.

Shiva's son Ganesha is corpulent and has an elephant head. He embodies the world of success, wealth, food and nourishment. Shiva's other son, Kartikeya, has six heads and holds a spear in his hand. He rides the peacock. He is the quintessential hero god, the warrior god, the warlord who defeats demons. Together, they bring in prosperity and peace. In Hinduism, the word for prosperity is 'labh'. For peaceful, auspicious prosperity the word is 'shubh-labh'. Another word for this is 'mangala'.

So, when Shiva and Shakti come together, they create a world that is prosperous and peaceful. The prosperity and the peace they bring together is imbued with wisdom. There is an understanding that a happy world is not one where there is only food for satisfying us or weapons to protect us, but a world where there is no fear or hunger. It is not only about acquiring wealth to satisfy hunger. It is not only about acquiring power to protect ourselves. It is about outgrowing hunger and fear.

This theme of outgrowing hunger and fear is represented through the animals associated with this family. You see a snake around Shiva's neck, but this snake is not attacking the rat that is associated with Ganesha. Similarly, the peacock, which is associated with Kartikeya, is not eating the snake that is associated with Shiva. So, the peacock does not attack the serpent. The serpent does not attack the rat. The rat does not attack the plate of sweets in Ganesha's hand. Nobody is attacking anybody because no one is hungry.

But hunger is outgrown. When the predator's hunger is outgrown, it does not threaten the prey and the prey is not frightened. In fact, the relation between the predator and prey ceases to exist when hunger is outgrown. For there is no fear and there is friendship. This is what the Shiva parivaar embodies. A world where there is no fear and no hunger; where there is enough food and power to provide us with prosperity, peace and auspiciousness.

Water Sprinkler
Silver
19th century, south India
H-190, W-95, D-95 mm

The colonial era saw the advent of decorative silver table ornaments popular amongst both Europeans and the wealthy Indians. An innovation on the traditional water lota or Gangajali, this silver water sprinkler had a piston mechanism which, when pumped, sprayed water from the four raised flowers. The elaborately decorated object uses a combination of repoussé, casting, wire-binding and soldering in its manufacture, finished with gilding to present a two-tone effect. The central part of the vessel has cartouches containing floral decorations besides attendant figures blowing the conch alongside Ganesha and Kartikeya, the offspring of Shiva and Parvati. A slender neck decorated by two parrots is surmounted by a finial in the sculpted form of Shiva and Parvati on Mt. Kailash. This highly sculptural object is a tour-de-force of silver smithy both in its design and ingenious water mechanism.

vishnu

Vishnu is called the preserver of the universe. He is, however, not preserving the world. He is preserving life. He is part of the Hindu trinity with Brahma and Shiva and, in fact, resolves the tension between them. Brahma creates life. Therefore, hunger and fear. Shiva, the hermit, seeks to destroy hunger and fear. In doing so, Shiva destroys life itself. Balance has to be achieved, and this balance is achieved through Vishnu. He enables the individual, the self, to outgrow hunger, by enabling 'the other' to get food and security. Thus, he is associated with creating the ideal social structure.

Shiva is the hermit who withdraws from society. Brahma is the householder who establishes society. Vishnu is the one who creates a happy society, free of conflict and strife. In the Vedas, Vishnu is linked to cows, to the ability to take three steps. He is considered the younger brother of Indra. While his role in the Vedas is very limited, it expands in the Puranic tradition, where he becomes the preserver. Here, he is found in two forms: the sleeping and the awakened form.

Hindus worship Vishnu as Narayana, the sleeping Vishnu, or as the four-armed Vishnu, in the seated or standing position, or his various avatars, especially the Dashavatar. These avatars are also worshipped as local deities in local places. For example, Shrinathji is worshiped in Nathdwara, Rajasthan, and Pandurang is worshipped in Maharashtra. These are regional forms of Vishnu. In it, the deity is seen as residing in that particular temple. Unlike Vishnu's avatars that are transcendental and belong everywhere, deities like Shrinathji and Panduranga have a geographical anchoring. They played an important role in the rise of temple culture, agrarian economies and the Bhakti movements that were rooted to the ground

In fact, it is said that Hinduism became popular and Buddhism waned in significance because Buddha remained a transcendental figure, who existed in the distant past and was not anchored to geography. While the Brahmins located folk gods, village gods, clan gods that came to be identified with the transcendental Vishnu. Thus, folk could connect to Vishnu's universality. This also led to the rise of pilgrim spots across India, especially from the

Puranic period, where every village came to be associated with a deity. Pilgrim routes were established. Through them, local manifestations of the divine came to be connected with the universal manifestation. People travelled the length and breadth of India visiting various deities. This process connected the deities and created a Pilgrim Nation.

Wayside and subsidiary shrines frequently depicted gods as icons on the wall, usually in the form of plaques with just a rendition of the face, enough for the faithful to recognise and identify them. This icon of Vishnu is rendered in the repoussé technique. His neck and crown have a variety of patterns and shapes in tiers, which have been carved and etched with great attention to detail. Two rounded loops on either side of the crown enable anchoring the image to the shrine. Filled with lac from the back to protect the icon's form, it is further sealed by a copper sheet layer. For its shape and size, the object is unusually heavy.

Vishnu Plaque
Silver, copper
19th century, Deccan Plateau
H-395, W-170, D-30 mm

narayana

The sleeping form of Vishnu is called Narayana. He is the one who goes into deep slumber. When he sleeps this dreamless sleep, the world does not exist. When he awakens, the world comes into being. When he sleeps again, the world ceases to be. Thus, the sleeping Vishnu is a metaphor for our consciousness. When the consciousness withdraws into itself, the world ceases to be. The world exists only when we are awake. This is a reference to subjectivity.

Our world exists when we exist. Our world ceases to be when we are asleep. Our world does not exist when we die. However, the world continues to exist. The sleeping Vishnu is visualised as lying on an ocean of milk, in the coils of a multi-hooded serpent. The ocean of milk is a metaphor for the material world, which contains all life and energy. One can churn everything that one desires from this milk. Just as from milk we can extract butter, we can extract wealth and power from nature.

The serpent represents time. Its coils indicate that time is at a standstill. When Vishnu awakens, the serpent will uncoil. It is then used to churn the ocean milk. From this ocean, all things emerge that we bring into our lives: responsibility, success, pleasure and, eventually, wisdom.

This unique fragment, a silver plaque depicting Narayana (Vishnu) in Anantyasana on the serpent Shesha, is seen flanked by Lakshmi. Surrounding figures paying obeisance are possibly meant to represent the donors of the object. The work of skilled artisans, the iconographic elements of this tiny votive are impressive not only for their fidelity to detail but also for the delicate modelling and chiselling of figures, raised elements of design and subtle gilding. This double-sided piece depicts on its verso Vishnu as Krishna, vanquishing Kaliya, the demon snake, flanked by the snake's wives and attendants pleading forgiveness.

Votive Fragment
Silver, gold
18th century, south India
H-59, W-86, D-12 mm

narasimha

Narasimha is an avatar of Vishnu. There was once a demon who had received a boon. He could not be killed by anyone who was either human or animal, at day or at night, inside or outside, on the ground or in the sky. To kill this demon, Vishnu took the form of Narasimha, which is neither man nor animal. He emerged from a pillar and that set him apart from all living creatures, as all living creatures are born from either the womb or the egg.

Narasimha appeared at twilight, which is neither day nor night, and carried the demon to the threshold, which is neither inside nor outside. He placed the demon on his upraised thigh, which was neither on the ground nor in the sky. Thus, having fulfilled all conditions, Narasimha ripped open the demon's gut, pulled out his entrails and drank his blood. In doing so, he rescued the demon's son, Prahlada. Prahlada believed in the possibilities of life and rejected the idea that his father was the most powerful being on Earth. He is the archetypal devotee and is thus associated with Narasimha.

Narasimha reminds us of a very strong Hindu idea: everything in the world is never known to the human mind. The human mind is limited, while nature is unlimited. Nature will always defy us by breaking categories, and by mingling and merging the various boxed realities of our existence.

Small silver plaques across India frequently surprise us with the enormous regional myths and legends they pack in. Their iconographic details are an indicator of the communities who used and frequently worshipped them. This plaque, in great graphic detail, depicts the moment when Vishnu as Narasimha rips apart the guts of demon Hiranyakashyapu flanked by attendant figures. The figures depicted are slightly raised and chiselled in the outline with a few basic decorative flourishes. The words 'Narasimha Avatar' in rudimentary Devanagari script have been lightly carved above the lion's head.

Plaque
Silver
19th century, north India
H-82, W-100, D-13 mm

ram

Ram is one of the most powerful and popular avatars of Vishnu. He is born as the eldest son in a royal family of the solar dynasty. On the eve of his coronation, he is exiled to the forest for fourteen years, while his brother is made king. Ram accepts this decision without any remorse and spends his time in the forest wandering from the hermitage of one sage to another.

In the final year of his exile, his wife is abducted by a rakshasa called Ravan, who has an island kingdom in the middle of the sea. Ram is able to raise an army of monkeys and bears and birds, build a bridge across the sea and attack the city of Lanka, to defeat the rakshasas and rescue his wife, Sita, who he brings back to Ayodhya.

This story is retold in the epic, Ramayana, composed by Valmiki, which has been translated to almost every Indian language. In the story, Ram is valourised as the ideal king because he values his people's opinion over his own and because he obeys the king without question.

Thus, he is the ideal king, who listens to people, and the ideal subject, who listens to the king. He is considered to be the embodiment of atma because he wants nothing. All his actions are driven by a sense of duty. He is called Maryada Purushotam, the exemplar of rule following. He always follows the rules, even when he knows that justice is not being achieved. This is because rules matter to him and he believes that rules create order. It is through rules, suffering its negative and positive qualities, that a great society is established.

His kingdom, known Ram Rajya, is considered to be the world where all things are in order and everything happens predictably.

Ram Durbar
Silver
19th century, north India/ Deccan Plateau
H-370, W-258, D-6 mm

Popularly known as Ram Durbar, or the court of Ram, this composition of figures is usually placed within private shrines. Under a torana-like engraved arch, topped by a Kirtimukha and surmounted by a royal parasol, stands the figure of Ram, his wife Sita and brother Lakshman, flanked by two attendants. Bharat and Shatrughna, his other brothers, flank the central figures while Hanuman is seen seated at Ram's feet. The dismantlable shrine and figures were cast in a mould with details subsequently carved and etched onto their surface. The sculptures rest on a curved and decorated plinth on four lion claws to give a niche-like appearance to the edifice. The maker's artistry emerges when we note that the gentle gradation in size and scale of the statues and their decorative detail keep our attention on the entire ensemble rather than on any one figure.

krishna

Krishna complements Ram. Both are mortal forms of Vishnu born on Earth to establish dharma. But they belong to different contexts. Ram is born in an earlier age, the Treta yuga. Krishna is born in a latter age, the Kali yuga. Ram is an elite; the eldest son of a royal family. Krishna, while born in a royal family, is brought up as the youngest son of a cowherd. Ram becomes king. Krishna is a kingmaker. Both strive for dharma—enabling the strong to help the weak, with love, that is, without the need to turn the world into an ecosystem of victims, villains and heroes.

The Bhagavata Purana and the Mahabharata tell the story of Krishna. It is retold in various folktales, too. Krishna has three most common forms: one, as the baby Krishna in the cradle; two, as a cowherd and flautist, with Radha, surrounded by gopikas; and finally, Krishna the charioteer, giving the lessons of the Gita to Arjun, at the start of the battle at Kurukshetra.

The Bhagavata Purana focuses on the early life of Krishna as a child in a village of cowherds and milkmaids. Here, he is a prankster, the village protector and the rake who enchants the women with his charm and beauty and the sound of his flute.

The Mahabharata section begins with Krishna participating and winning a wrestling match in Mathura. He kills Mathura's dictator, Kansa. He then realises he is a member of the royal clan of Yadavas, of the lunar dynasty. He was raised in secret, for it was feared that he would be killed by Kansa. However, the killing of Kansa has a horrific consequence.

Kansa's father-in-law, Jarasandha, attacks the city of Mathura. He sets it aflame, forcing Krishna and the Yadavas to travel westwards, across the desert. They find refuge in the island city of Dwarka. From thence, Krishna deals with the kings in his neighbourhood. He manages to overcome any opposition he faces.

Krishna marries princesses from the kingdoms of Madra, Kekaya, Avanti and Kosala. By marrying these eight queens, he becomes very powerful. He supports the Pandavas of the Kuru clan. In exchange for defeating the

Kauravas, the Pandavas help Krishna by killing Jarasandha in a duel. He thus avenges the destruction of Mathura.

The great Mahabharata war is where Krishna plays the role of a political advisor to the Pandavas. He enables them to establish justice, without hating the perpetrators of the crime. Thus, he establishes the concept of dharma, where people who abuse the weak, that is, Kansa, Jarasandha and Duryodhana, are overthrown.

The Mahabharata section of Krishna's life is rather masculine, brutal and violent. It lacks the romance, the femininity and the joy of the earlier part of his life. These two halves of Krishna's life—the childhood and youth followed by his days as a statesman—make him a powerful being in Hindu mythology.

In the end, the mother of the Kauravas curses Krishna. She states that he will witness the death of his entire clan, helplessly. Krishna, too, accepts this curse with grace. He does not use his divine powers to change the fate of his own clan.

Like Ram, Krishna struggles to establish dharma on Earth. Unlike Ram, he bends the rules in the pursuit of dharma. Like Ram, he has to confront tyrants but he never hates them, and always treats them with respect, hoping they will see the folly of their ways. Unlike Ram, Krishna knows he is Vishnu on Earth. He has knowledge of infinity. Yet, he has to function in a finite context. Like Ram, he has to deal with human weakness. Unlike Ram, he is known also for his romantic and artistic side, which is why he is popularly called 'purna avatar' or the complete incarnation.

Pendant
Silver
20th century, Nathdwara, western India
H-136, W-98, D-21 mm

Krishna in his manifestation of Shrinathji is traditionally worshipped in shrines with large cloth backings that depict him in a variety of seasonal and ritual forms. This pendant, shaped like an inverted cusped arch, has the iconic image of Shrinathji chased in repoussé with added vegetal and floral motifs. Bunches of small silver balls suspended add a touch of delicacy and create a gentle rustling sound when worn. Silversmiths were quick to tap into religious sentiments by creating souvenirs that were carried from pilgrimage sites as keepsakes for family members who couldn't make the trip.

jaya vijaya

Jaya and Vijaya are doorkeepers of Vaikuntha, the abode of Vishnu. Their form is like Vishnu's, except that they have the shankra, chakra and gadha, but not the padma. The lotus flower is absent. They are shown in Abhay Mudra and they are mirror images of each other.

Across mythology, all gods have some doorkeepers. For example, Bhairava and Pisacha are the doorkeepers of Shiva. They look like Shiva. Maya and Laya are the doorkeepers of the goddess. Again, the doorkeepers are found in mirror images. The doorkeepers are always shown with fangs, to show they are demonic. Like any gatekeeper, they have the dual task of keeping people out and letting some people in, which does not make them people's favourites.

There are stories of how sages curse Jaya and Vijaya because they prevent them from entering Vaikuntha while Vishnu is sleeping. As a result, they are born on Earth first as yakshas, Hiranyaksha and Hiranyakashyapu. Then as rakshasas, such as Ravan and Kumbakarna. Then, as nasty human beings, such as Shishupal and Dantavakra. Thus, we see their fall for doing their duties.

In south Indian temples, Jaya and Vijaya also exist outside the door to remind us how great Vishnu himself is. Just looking at the doorkeepers we are made aware of how great the gods are. In earlier times, all communities were not allowed to enter certain temples. The people who were considered to be of lower castes had to satisfy themselves by looking at the image of the doorkeepers. They could then imagine how the deity within would have looked.

Offerings are also made to doorkeepers. This is an important part of Hindu tradition. It is a reminder that you cannot access anyone in a position of power without making people around them happy.

This Vaishnava private shrine depicts identical figures of Jaya and Vijaya carved on its door panels. Chased in the repoussé technique with added details engraved and etched, the panels would have been backed onto wooden frames and attached to the shrine's door. A wealth of Western decorative motifs entered Indian art forms in the 19th century. While the guardian figures of Jaya and Vijaya are Indic, they are surmounted by swags of European proscenium curtains in trefoil arches set within cartouches and bands of scrolling pattern, combining Eastern and Western decorative traditions.

Door Panels
Silver
19th century, south India
H-299, W-109, D-11 mm; H-300, W-110, D-11 mm

chanwar

Chanwar is a yak-tail fly whisk. It is used to keep away flies, but it is a symbol of royalty. In Sikhism, it is also used for the holy book, the Granth Sahib. This declared that the Sikh kings were merely stewards or regents. The real authority rested with the Holy Book or the Granth Sahib that contains the words of wisdom that takes us towards God.

The chanwar is used for kings like Ram and it is an expression of royal authority. In traditional society, the king was given a chanwar. The Viceroy would be given a morchap, a fan made of peacock feathers. Someone at a junior position was given a rumaal or a fan made of cloth. Thus, hierarchy was established using a chanwar.

Chanwar/ Fly Whisk
Silver, enamel, yak hair
19th century, north India
H-259 (without hair), H-629 (with hair), W-53, D-52 mm

An essential part of worship across religions, the chanwar and other religious accoutrements were used every day during rituals, leaving us with very few surviving examples of this quality. The silver handle moulded in shape and engraved at its extremities ends in a sphere. The other end with a wider opening is used to attach the yak hair. The object is completely enamelled with a design of peacocks, flowers and shrubs in tones of green, blue and red, a traditional palette popular in western India.

amulet

A talisman or an amulet contains something like ash or an offering made to a deity. It can be a flower or a leaf, or maybe a verse from a holy book. It contains the power of the holy object. This is called contagious magic whereby the power of the holy object or the deity is transferred to the talisman. Thus, it is transferred to the person wearing it. It is placed around the neck, waist or arm. This is found in both Hindu and Islamic traditions.

Amulet/ Armband
Silver
19th century, north India
H-89, W-90, D-50 mm

This amulet worn as an armband invokes the names of the Prophet and his immediate family (Mohammad, Ali, Fatima, Hassan, Hussain) in 'the name of Allah, the most gracious and the most merciful'. The calligraphy is engraved in the repoussé technique, with further detailing by chiselling and die-stamping. The connecting links and chains are hammered into shape, braided and then soldered onto the main piece. The screw-type hinge is surmounted by a delicately shaped lotus bud. The inscriptions indicate a previous Shia Muslim provenance to the object.

book stand

Holy books like the Quran were never placed on the ground, in India. They were covered with cloth and placed on special holders to read them. Since binding was not a very popular practice in Medieval times, the books had loose papers, either made from leaf, cloth or metal. It later became paper. Paper was later introduced in 13th century India by the Persianised Turks.

The holy books were written in various scripts and profusely illustrated. They were sometimes even gilded and kept at very important positions. There were special rooms made for the holy books. They were treated as deities. They were worshipped during festival times and read out to the community. The special book holder, thus, had great importance in local traditions.

These practices were popularised after the arrival of the Persianised Turks. For them, the Holy Quran became important. As a result of which even Hindu communities started valuing books much more than the previous generations. Thus, the Bhagavata Purana and the Ramayana were being written since the 10th century onwards. They were also worshipped in special places. The Bhagavata Purana, the Bhagavad Gita and the Ramayana were given the same importance in Hindu households as the Quran was given in Muslim households. The Guru Granth Sahib became important in the Sikh traditions. These are indicative of the enormous influence Islamic traditions had in India. This tells us how books became part of religious practices in India over time, a concept that did not exist in ancient times.

Rehal/ Book Stand
Jade, gold
17th–18th century, north India
H-168, W-150, D-90 mm

Carved from a single block of Nephrite Jade, the two equal-sized panels of the book stand slide into a permanent bind. The stand's exterior is detailed with geometric trellis patterns with its outlines highlighted in gold. The legs and finials of the stand are designed to resemble lobed archways invoking Islamic architecture. The object, a fine example of decorative restrain, would have been used to hold the Holy Quran while it was being read.

Acknowledgements

This book is the result of several years of research and collaborative planning. We thank Devdutt Pattanaik for his invigorating analysis of the objects in our collection, which has today enabled us to share a nuanced understanding of this treasure with the world.

As the series editor of our current publication programme, we thank Pramod Kumar KG of Eka Archiving for holding this endeavour together.

For the remarkable quality of images reproduced here, we thank Umesh Gogna for his photography and Prateeksha K. Tholia for image styling. We gratefully acknowledge the dedication and support of Surbhi Mathur at Amrapali Museum and Ramya Sharma at Amrapali Jewels, besides other colleagues at both institutions who have helped make this book a reality. This project would not have been realised but for the steadfast custodianship of this collection by Neeru Arora, Tarang and Akanksha Arora. Their support through this project has been our biggest strength.

Rajesh Ajmera & Rajiv Arora